STUDIES IN PUBLIC CHOICE

Studies in Public choice

Vol. 1

Editor: Gordon Tullock

The intersection of economics and politics

The intersection of economics and politics is one of the most important areas of modern social science. *Public Choice*, as a journal, and the series, Studies in Public Choice, are devoted to a particularly important aspect of this intersection, the use of economic methods on matters which are traditionally political. Prominent scholars, such as Duncan Black, Kenneth Arrow, Mancur Olson, Vincent Ostrom, and James Buchanan, have contributed to the development of the study of public choice; notably some were originally economists and some political scientists. The journal *Public Choice* (now in its twelfth year) and the monograph series are devoted to furthering the growth of knowledge in this important and fascinating field.

Fiscal responsibility in constitutional democracy

James M. Buchanan
and
Richard E. Wagner

Virginia Polytechnical Institute and State University

Martinus Nijhoff Social Sciences Division
Leiden | Boston 1978

Distributors for North America
Kluwer Boston, Inc.
160 Old Derby Street
Hingham, MA 02043 USA

ISBN 90.207.0743.4

Printed in the Netherlands by Intercontinental Graphics

PREFACE

This volume contains the papers, along with the discussant's remarks, presented at a conference on 'Federal Fiscal Responsibility', held at The Homestead, Hot Springs, Virginia, on 26-27 March 1976. Additionally, we, the editors, have included an introductory essay which sets forth some of our background thoughts that informed our organization of the conference and which also describes some of our reactions to the conference.

This conference was sponsored by the Liberty Fund, Inc. of Indianapolis, Indiana, which incorporated this conference into its overall program directed toward the study of the ideals of a free society of responsible individuals. Related to this effort, the Liberty Fund also assisted in supporting research on *Democracy in Deficit: The Political Legacy of Lord Keynes*, by James M. Buchanan and Richard E. Wagner (New York: Academic Press, 1977). Both *Democracy in Deficit* and the conference were designed to examine one important aspect of the Liberty Fund's general set of concerns, namely the way in which political considerations influence the macroeconomic aspects of budgetary policy, thereby, in turn, influencing the future of American liberty and prosperity. We are most grateful to the Liberty Fund for their efforts, and we are pleased that Enid Goodrich, William Fletcher, Neil McLeod, and Helen Schultz of the Liberty Fund were able to attend the conference.

The organization of the conference was handled through the Center for Study of Public Choice, specifically through the cheerful and capable efforts of Mrs. Betty T. Ross. For her graciousness and generosity, we are exceedingly grateful. This volume is published in the Public Choice Monograph Series, and we are thankful to Gordon Tullock, editor of the series, for his helpfulness. The general theme of *Fiscal Responsibility in Constitutional Democracy* is, of course, quite pertinent to the theme of this series.

Armen A. Alchian, University of California, Los Angeles
William Breit, University of Virginia
Martin Bronfenbrenner, Duke University
James M. Buchanan, Virginia Polytechnic Institute and State
   University
Jesse Burkhead, Syracuse University
Colin Campbell, Dartmouth College
Otto A. Davis, Carnegie-Mellon University
Marilyn R. Flowers, University of Oklahoma
Donald F. Gordon, Simon Fraser University
C. Lowell Hariss, Columbia University
Thomas F. Johnson, American Enterprise Institute
Charles Knerr, University of Texas at Arlington
J. Clayburn LaForce, University of California, Los Angeles
Abba P. Lerner, Queen's College, City University of New York
William H. Meckling, University of Rochester
David Meiselman, Virginia Polytechnic Institute and State
   University
Michael E. Levy, The Conference Board, Inc.
William A. Niskanen, Ford Motor Company
Mancur Olson, University of Maryland
Alan Reynolds, First National Bank of Chicago
Warren J. Samuels, Michigan State University
Wilson E. Schmidt, Virginia Polytechnic Institute and State
   University

Herbert Stein, University of Virginia
Robert D. Tollison, Virginia Polytechnic Institute and State University
Gordon Tullock, Virginia Polytechnic Institute and State University
Melville J. Ulmer, University of Maryland
Richard E. Wagner, Virginia Polytechnic Institute and State University
Burton A. Weisbrod, University of Wisconsin
Edwin G. West, Carleton University

CONTENTS

1. CONTEMPORARY DEMOCRACY AND THE PROSPECT FOR FISCAL CONTROL: INITIAL THOUGHTS ABOUT AND FINAL REACTIONS TO THE CONFERENCE

James M. Buchanan and Richard E. Wagner

The driving motivations behind the conference on Federal Fiscal Responsibility were an interest in the reasons for and a concern about the long-term consequences of a dramatic shift in the pattern of American fiscal history that occurred during the second quarter of this century. Before the 1930s, budget surpluses were the dominant state of affairs; budget deficits have since come to dominate our fiscal life. The budget surpluses that were so normal prior to the Great Depression of the 1930s were used to amortize the federal debt that was created during times of war and recession. The federal government customarily resorted to deficit finance to pay for wars and to offset declining taxes during recessionary periods, but during normal periods the government redeemed this debt with surpluses of taxes over expenditures. In the years immediately following the creation of the American Republic, the federal budget was nearly always in deficit. As this tumultuous period drew to a close, the nation found itself saddled with a debt of $83.8 million, quite a substantial sum for those days. In response, Congress enacted the Sinking Fund Act of 1795. This act provided for budget surpluses to be generated, with the proceeds used to retire the national debt. Budget deficits once again ensued following the Panic of 1837, but with budget surpluses generally resulting thereafter until the Civil War. Between the Civil War and World War I, surpluses once again dominated budgetary policy, with the proceeds being used to reduce the national debt. And debt reduction prevailed after World War I until the onset of the Great

Depression. With the Great Depression, this uniform, recurring pattern of fiscal history — deficits created during recessions and wars, with surpluses created during normal times to amortize the national debt — ceased.

Budget deficits prevailed and public debt accumulated during the Great Depression just as was true for the earlier recessionary periods. And when World War II followed on the heels of the depression, the pattern of deficit finance and debt accumulation continued, again just as was true for other wartime periods. But with the cessation of hostilities and the return to peace and prosperity, the former budgetary pattern did not return in its full vigor. During this postwar period and running throughout the presidency of Dwight Eisenhower, an approximate pattern of budget balance prevailed. Deficits in some years were offset by surpluses in other years, but no serious effort was made to reduce the amount of national debt. The post-war level of public debt was largely accepted as permanent, and efforts were directed not at reducing this debt but at keeping it from increasing. The fading of our former, long-standing budgetary pattern had begun.

A new budgetary pattern, which may be called Keynesian, as against the earlier, Classical pattern, emerged in the 1960s, and can be principally dated from the tax cut of 1964. Our budgetary history since then has been one of almost continual deficit. Democracy in deficit has come to describe aptly our recent fiscal experience. Now, balanced budgets are envisioned during periods of full employment, with budget deficits resulting otherwise. This shift in budgetary pattern was a political consequence of the shift in generally-held understandings or beliefs about the nature of the economic order, as well as about the value of adherence to such alternative budgetary precepts as the Classical and the Keynesian. While the etiology of this shift in budgetary patterns is explored in our book *Democracy in Deficit: The Political Legacy of Lord Keynes*,[1] a brief description would seem in order at this time because it was our initial, inchoate belief in the applicability of this theme that motivated the formation of the conference in the first place.

---

1. New York: Academic Press, 1977. For an extension of our thesis to the United Kingdom, see James M. Buchanan, Richard E. Wagner, and John Burton, *The Consequences of Mr. Keynes* (London: Institute for Economic Affairs, forthcoming).

Anyone, citizens as well as politicians, typically would like to live beyond their means. Individual citizens generally face a budget constraint which prevents them from acting on this desire, although some people counterfeit and others go bankrupt. Before the shift in understanding wrought by the Keynesian revolution, politicians acted as if they sensed a similar constraint when making the nation's budgetary choices. During this earlier period, our free enterprise economy was regarded as being essentially stable in the manner described by Say's Equality.[2] While fluctuations in economic activity would occur in such an economy, these fluctuations would set in motion self-correcting forces. Within this economic framework, the best action for government was for it to avoid injecting additional sources of instability into the economy. Avoiding such sources of instability, along with keeping debt and taxes low so as to promote thrift and saving was the way to achieve prosperity.

The Keynesian message created, by contrast, an image of, or belief in an inherently unstable economy, one that is as likely to be saddled with substantial unemployment as it is to provide full employment. Prosperity, according to this vision, could be assured only through conscious efforts of government to keep the economy performing at its peak, to help the economy to avoid the buffeting forces of inflation and recession. The Keynesian message, in other words, contained two central features. One was the image of an inherently unstable economy, one that was not governed by some "natural law" of a generally smooth coordination of economic activities. The other feature was the view of government as having both the obligation and the ability to offset this instability so as to bring about a more smoothly functioning economic order.

While Lord Keynes published his *General Theory* in 1936, his presuppositions did not infuse themselves into generally held understandings or beliefs for about a generation, much as he himself had observed as the lag in time between the articulation of an idea and the time when that idea became influential, given that it will become influential at all. While the Keynesian visions of the nature of our economic order and the proper pattern of budgetary policy gained dominance in academia in the 1940s and 1950s, they did not

2. For a recent statement of this perspective, see W. H. Hutt, *A Rehabilitation of Say's Law* (Athens: Ohio University Press, 1974).

filter into the general climate of opinion until the 1960s. With this conversion or shift in generally held perspectives or beliefs, macroeconomic engineering became the province of government.[3]

As developed by the economists who advocated macroeconomic engineering, fiscal policy would be devoted to smoothing out cycles in private economic activity. Fiscal policy would be guided by the same principle during both recession and inflation. Deficits would be created during recession and surpluses during inflation, both with the objective of smoothing out peaks and troughs. There was little awareness that the dictates of political survival might run contrary to the requirements of macroeconomic engineering, assuming for now that the economic order is aptly described by the Keynesian paradigm. That is, the political survival of politicians was tacitly assumed automatically to be strengthened as they came to follow more fully the appropriate fiscal policies.

But contemporary political institutions – constrained by a general belief in the Keynesian vision – do not operate in this symmetical manner. While there is little political resistance to budget deficits, there is substantial resistance to budget surpluses. Hence, fiscal policy will tend to be applied asymmetrically: deficits will be created frequently but surpluses will materialize only rarely. The explanation for this bias resides in the shift in the general, public impression or understanding of our economic order, and of the related rules of thumb held generally by the citizenry as to what constitutes prudent, reasonable, or efficacious conduct by government as regards its budget. Old-fashioned beliefs about the appropriateness of balanced budget norms and of redeeming public debt during periods of normalcy became undermined, and they lost their hold upon the public. In consequence, debt retirement lost its claim as a guiding norm. As a result, budget surpluses lost their raison d'être. In this new setting, surpluses had little survival value. Deficits allow politicians to increase spending without having directly and forthrightly to raise taxes. There is little obstacle to such a policy. Surpluses, on the other hand, require government to raise taxes without increasing spending – a program far more capable of generating political opposition than budget deficits, especially once the constraining norm of debt

---

3. For a thorough survey of this shift in paradigm toward fiscal policy, see Herbert Stein, *The Fiscal Revolution in America* (Chicago: University of Chicago Press, 1969).

retirement had receded from public consciousness.

These political biases toward budget deficits become also a bias toward inflation. This inflationary bias becomes apparent once it is recognized that monetary institutions as they are currently constituted will to some extent operate to increase the stock of money in response to deficits. But this inflationary bias can be considerably more destructive than a simple increase in the price of products and services, once it is recognized that the ensuing shifts in the structure of prices exacerbate the mistakes made in economic calculation. People will act on the basis of price signals that are inconsistent with the underlying structure of preferences and technology. As a result of these mistakes, decisions will be made regarding investment and the employment of resources that are not sustainable by the economy. Consequently, unemployment and capital waste will result as people come to readjust their plans and actions in response to the realization of these mistakes based on erroneous signals in the economy.[4]

The distortion in the structure of production that follows from inflation suggests in turn the possibility that the political implementation of Keynesian prescriptions may create a type of self-fulfilling prophecy. An inherently stable economy as described by Say's Equality undergoes a shift in budget policy due to a shift in the nature of the general understanding of or beliefs about the economic order. A general policy of a non-interventionist fiscal policy designed in normal times to retire public debt becomes replaced by an interventionist fiscal policy required to balance the economy, only with a bias toward deficits. This particular mix of policies that emerges leads in turn to economic instability because of the mistaken, non-sustainable employment of resources. The biased application of budgetary policies creates economic instability, only the instability is taken to confirm the Keynesian view of the unstable character of the economic order. The entire process is much like the formerly standard treatment of bleeding patients in certain instances. The condition of patients subject to such treatment often continued to deteriorate, and this continued deterioration often was interpreted as a sign that further bleeding was needed.

---

4. For an elaboration of this theme as it relates to the scope for political business cycles, see Richard E. Wagner, "Economic Manipulation for Political Profit: Macroeconomic Consequences and Constitutional Implications," *Kyklos* 30 (No. 3, 1977), 395-410.

This précis of *Democracy in Deficit* described our central thoughts about current economic policy as we organized the conference on Federal Fiscal Responsibility; this is true even though the planning of the conference preceded our writing of the book. Our idea for the conference was to have papers on three general aspects of our theme. First, we would have papers on the historical development of budgetary policy and ideas about such policy. The idea here would be to examine the shift both in budgetary policy and in thought about such policy. Second, we would have papers that diagnosed the present situation, papers that presented differing interpretations of Keynesian economics in a democratic setting. Third, we would have papers looking toward the future, papers that would examine efforts to deal with fiscal responsibility. With this organizational format in mind, we selected two papers for each of these three sessions, and also selected two discussants for each paper.

With respect to the first session on history, William Breit's "Starving the Leviathan: Balanced Budget Prescriptions before Keynes" examines the importance attached to budget balancing, to traditional or old-fashioned rules of sound finance in the pre-Keynesian period. The second paper, by Herbert Stein, "The Decline of Budget Balancing, Or How the Good Guys Finally Lost" explores the emergence of Keynesian prescriptions within our political-fiscal order. This paper presents themes and further reflections from his massive history of fiscal policy in America, *The Fiscal Revolution in America.*

The second session, on the contemporary setting, contained one paper in support of the Keynesian prescriptions and one paper suggesting that the Keynesian message has been harmful. Abba P. Lerner's "Keynesianism: Alive, If not so Well at Forty" defends and restates the elementary Keynesian ascription about the nature of our economic order. It also reiterates the Keynesian or functional finance view of the role of government in such an economic order. James M. Buchanan and Richard E. Wagner's "The Political Biases of Keynesian Economics" explores, along lines suggested above, the asymmetrical application of Keynesian prescriptions that is likely to emerge under prevailing democratic institutions, and offers a rationale for some form of constitutional amendment to require balanced budgets and stable monetary growth.

The third session, on future prospects and methods for fiscal control, contained one paper suggesting that the problem of control was essentially a legislative matter, one, moreover, that had already been brought under some measure of control, and another paper suggesting that the fundamental problem lies precisely in the need for constitutional reform of our political order. Jesse Burkhead and Charles Knerr's "Congressional Budget Reform: New Decision Structures" describes and offers some assessment of the likely impact of the Congressional Budget Act of 1974. This act was intended to bring the federal budget under greater control, and the authors give a generally sympathetic and optimistic assessment of this effort. William A. Niskanen's "The Prospect for Liberal Democracy" sets forth a case for constitutional reform as a necessary means of restoring a greater semblance of fiscal responsibility. In Niskanen's framework, there are defects in the prevailing constitutional order which make the attainment of fiscal responsibility essentially impossible without such constitutional reform.

These papers, along with the discussants' remarks, indicate a variety of outlooks and positions. This was our intent. At the same time, however, we were somewhat surprised by the meager support for our own position that the conduct of our budgetary policy has been following dangerous paths, and that we should be concerned about the course that events have been taking. Our view that the former constitutional order has been rescinded by the ascendency of Keynesian economics and its superstructure of ideas, norms, and values found little support, and the same coolness greeted our suggestion that explicit constitutional reform was desirable at this time. Instead, the common attitude was pretty much one of business as usual. While the economic situation was not regarded as generally ideal, it was not felt that there was anything fundamentally awry in our economic order. On the whole, it was suggested once again that more enlightened economic advice would set matters right, although there was obvious disagreement over which economists can be trusted to give the most enlightened advice.

Needless to say, we do not accept this still-dominant, roseate projection. We should like to do so, but our reading of the evidence does not allow us to be so sanguine. President Carter, of course, believes in balanced budgets, and he tells us that such a state of affairs will be attained in 1981. This claim, of course, has been repeated continually since the tax cut of 1964. Now, as always, deficits are supported as being necessary in the short-run so as to promote a healthier, more buoyant economy in the long-run. The deficits road to surplus, however, remains much touted but seldom traveled.

While the prospects for fiscal control do not look bright at this time, we are not fatalists or determinists. As with the vision of Charles Dickens' Spirit of Christmas Yet-to-Come, future prospects look bleak only if existing modes of fiscal conduct are continued. It is precisely because we do not see one inevitable projection of history, but rather see existing at this moment alternative histories that might unfold, and which will unfold as a result of choice and the exercise of intelligence, that we see hope, hope that through the articulation of the potentially harmful consequences of present courses of action we shall choose courses of action that will allow us to escape from these consequences.[5] As people come to understand more accurately (or less accurately, for that matter) the source of difficulties that plague them, fiscal conduct will change correspondingly. We engaged in a process in which the explanation of social phenomena alters our understanding of our self-interest, thereby modifying human conduct, which in turn alters the phenomena observed. We hope that the recent signs of concern about federal fiscal conduct, of which this volume is one expression, will contribute to this needed shift in understanding and, resultantly, budgetary policy.

5. For a statement of this theme about intelligence and choice,, see Frank H. Knight, *Intelligence and Democratic Action* (Cambridge: Harvard University Press, 1960). See also G. Warren Nutter, *Where Are We Headed?* Reprint No. 34 (Washington: American Enterprise Institute, 1975), originally published in the *Wall Street Journal*, January 10, 1975.

2. STARVING THE LEVIATHAN: BALANCED BUDGET PRESCRIPTIONS BEFORE KEYNES

William Breit

> "And thou shalt lend unto many nations,
> but thou shalt not borrow."
> Deuteronomy 15:6

In his magisterial account of medicine in the ancient world, pathologist Guido Majno concluded that many nostrums and remedies for wounds prescribed by our primitive ancestors seemed to work although they did so for reasons that are not apparent on the surface. In many other aspects of their behavior, seemingly irrational practices are only later discovered to have had silent merit. One inscrutable activity was that of burning the skeleton of animals, treating the resulting configurations made in the charred remains as a map, and renewing the hunt the next day according to the patterns on the shoulder bone. Our ancestors believed that the gods showed them where to hunt through magic. But the real merit of this nonsense was that over-hunting in any single part of the territory was prevented. Their method randomized the hunt in a way that could not be improved upon by the modern computer. Thus they achieved long-run practical results that from their vantage point seemed magical.[1]

The dedication to the balanced budget rule by our Founding Father ancestors and almost all subsequent political leaders until the 1930s also had operative results that were not always the same as the ones proclaimed. For in effect, it significantly limited the size of the state. The leviathan that was leashed by the Constitution was kept in a weakened condition approaching starvation. Although the point was not understood at the time, the size of the state in a

---

1. Guido Majno, *The Healing Hand* (Cambridge: Harvard University Press, 1975).

democracy is inextricably linked to the possibility of deficit financing. At the constitutional level of choice a decision was made to keep government small relative to the private sector. The method proclaimed for achieving that end was clearly enumerated, limited powers. But the real limiting force on the size of the state was, until recent history, the mythology of budget-balancing.

The budget-balance rule was a constitutional constraint if we conceive of a "constitution" as a limitation on the power of lawmaking bodies, that is, a set of fixed principles antecedent to and controlling the operating institutions of government. The unique contribution of American constitutional thought was the notion of a written document enumerating the essential rights of individuals to serve as limits on the actions of legislators and courts. The written document of a Constitution clarified the important distinction between constitutional law and the law made by the ordinary legislature. It was believed that the Constitution was grounded in a fundamental source of authority higher than that which gives out temporary laws. This authority could be gained only if the Constitution were created by "an act of *all*".[2] Unanimity was the gound of higher authority legitimizing the Constitutional constraint on legislatures and courts.[3]

The balanced-budget rule which serves as a part · of the Constitution was, of course, not in the form of a written statement that every expenditure must be balanced by a tax. But it nevertheless had constitutional status. For expenditures in excess of receipts were considered to be in violation of moral principles. The imperative of the balanced budget was an extra-legal rule or custom that grew up around the formal document. It existed outside the precise letter of the Constitution on all fours with the system of political parties, the presidential cabinet, the actual operation of the electoral college system and the doctrine of judicial review. But its

2. Bernard Bailyn, *The Ideological Origins of the American Revolution* (Cambridge: The Belknap Press of Harvard University Press, 1967) p. 182. Bailyn is citing the author of *Four Letters On Interesting Subjects*, one of two pamphlets published in 1776 that represented "brilliant sparks thrown off by the clash of Revolutionary politics in Pennsylvania, [that] lit up the final steps of the path that led directly to the first constitutions of the American states."

3. Written constitutions had originated as commercial charters (for example, the charter of the Massachusetts Bay Colony) which essentially were a delegation of powers by the crown to enterprisers willing to undertake risks of exploration and settlement. In the colonial setting these changed in character and ultimately became the frame of government, Bailyn, *Ibid.*, p. 190.

constitutional status meant in practice that for a long time the representative man in American society perceived a contingent liability in the issuance of public debt instruments.

Even before the inauguration of the first president or the establishment of a treasury department it was recognized that the new republic must have some provision for raising public revenue. James Madison laid the subject before the House of Representatives in a bill providing for revenues through tariff measures. In 1789 a treasury department was established. It is significant that this institution was placed in a specially intimate relation to Congress independent of the President. Calls for financial information were to be made directly to the treasury department without going through the presidential office.[4] In this statute Congress placed the responsibility for the budget upon Congress, not upon the Executive, as was the established practice in all European countries at the time. In 1795 a standing committee on finance was established — the precursor of the later Ways and Means Committee — with the duty of reporting on the state of public debt, revenue and expenditures. Alexander Hamilton, the first Secretary of the Treasury, was not an enthusiastic supporter of public debt. Adam Smith's *Wealth of Nations* was an important source for his *Report on Manufactures* and influenced most of his state papers.[5] In Hamilton's characteristic words, "As the vicissitudes of nations begat a perpetual tendency to the accumulation of debt, there ought to be a perpetual, anxious, and unceasing effort to reduce that which at any time exists, as fast as shall be practicable, consistent with integrity and good faith."[6] Hamilton's views on public debt as stated in his reports on federal credit in 1790 and in 1795 argued that public and private debt are closely allied and inseparable and must be put into a manageable form. A balanced budget ultimately was the goal for only then could the credit of the United States be established.[7] The ability of the new nation to raise

4. Davis Rich Dewey, *Financial History of the United States* (New York: Longmans, Green and Co., 1931) pp. 85–89.
5. Vernon Louis Parrington, *Main Currents in American Thought*, Volume I (New York: Harcourt, Brace and Co., 1930) pp. 293–307.
6. Cited in Paul Studenski and Hermand E. Kroos, *Financial History of the United States* (New York: McGraw-Hill, 1952) p. 55.
7. For a compilation of Hamilton's main points regarding public debt including adversary and supporting views, see George Rogers Taylor, ed., *Hamilton and the National Debt* (Boston: D. C. Heath and Co., 1950).

funds abroad quickly in an emergency was a necessity and so, according to Hamilton, a balanced budget was of supreme importance in normal times. Hamilton's principle of a balanced-budget mentality in public finance was kept largely intact throughout the nineteenth century and extended well into the twentieth century.

Nothwithstanding the constitutional principle that spending and taxing are inseparable, the interdependence between the two decisions was not brought clearly to the surface. Expenditures were set by congressional committees imbued with philosophical and practical ideas about the importance of limited government. Customs duties provided the bulk of the revenues. So receipts typically outstripped expenditures. Indeed surpluses were far more often the problem than were deficits. These surpluses tended to hide the interdependence of the fiscal accounts. The lucrative nature of customs duties never required a careful weighing of expenditures against revenues. The upshot was that the uncertainties and contradictions that ordinarily might be predicted to emerge from a bifurcated fiscal procedure were minimized.

The strength of the constitutional rule imposed by the budget-balance norm can best be appreciated by a perusal of the ideas about deficit financing that politicians held for most of our nation's history. Those of us who live in Virginia have a special interest in Thomas Jefferson. Every school child learns that Mr. Jefferson was against large government. Yet he is associated with a massive increase in government expenditures during his presidency. The reason, of course, was the Louisiana Purchase. Its cost was the impressive (for that day) sum of $15 million. Of that amount, only $3,750,000 was paid for out of current revenues, and $11,250,000 was borrowed at 6% interest. But that fact should not be interpreted as a rejection of the balanced budget principle. In his second annual message to Congress he stressed the importance of discharging the national debt so as to bring about "the emancipation of our posterity from this mortal canker."[8] To Jefferson, one generation should not be allowed to bind another. "The earth always belongs to the living generation" he insisted. Just as every constitution and every law should expire at the end of 19 years (since if it be enforced longer, "it is an act of force and not of

8. Dumas Malone, *Jefferson and the Rights of Man* (Boston: Little, Brown) p. 179.

right") so too the public debt should be extinguishable roughly every twenty years. Of all the perils facing the nation, he said, "public debt is the greatest of the dangers to be feared."[9]

As Merrill Peterson has pointed out in his biography of Jefferson, "In the Jeffersonian scripture, debt and taxes were public evils of the first magnitude. They drained capital away from the mass of citizens, diverted it from productive enterprise, and supported a system of coercion, corruption, and privilege that was the bane of every government and necessarily fatal to a free one. 'Economy and liberty, profusion and servitude,'"[10]

Jefferson was persuaded that public money could not constitutionally be spent for public education, roads, rivers and canals. When he was faced with a surplus in the national accounts he wanted to use it to retire the existing debt. But debt retirement created a problem because the attempt to do so would have altered the terms on which creditors had lent the money. The quaint problem of what to do with surplus funds was recurrent throughout the century.

Much the same sentiments were expressed by the administrations following in close proximity to Jefferson's. To James Madison, James Monroe and John Quincy Adams the balanced budget was the chief maxim of sound finance.[11]

Perhps the strongest views on public debt were those held by Andrew Jackson. They are of particular interest because they went beyond the simple statements of morality and efficiency found in the earlier pronouncements of his predecessors. He represented the viewpoint of rural and frontier America regarding the morality of public debt. But his populist impulses stressed the special problem that arose because of what be perceived as a perverse redistribution of income from paying interest on the debt. To Jackson's mind, interest on public debt hurt the productive classes which he identified with the working classes. The bulk of revenues came from customs duties which in effect were a form of regressive taxation. The public debt, on the other hand, was in the hands of the

9. *Ibid.*, p. 291.
10. Merrill D. Peterson, *Thomas Jefferson and the New Nation* (New York: Oxford University Press, 1970) p. 687.
11. Brief summaries of the views of various presidents on deficit financing can be found in Lewis H. Kimmel, *Federal Budget and Fiscal Policy 1789-1958* (Washington, D. C.: The Brookings Institution, 1959).

relatively rich. So the combined effects of taxing to get the proceeds to pay interest to bond holders involved a redistribution from the poor to the rich. Furthermore, and consistent with Jefferson's arguments, Jackson stressed that the channeling of funds into public debt meant an increase in "unproductive capital", namely government services. Paying off the existing debt involved a transfer of funds from unproductive activities into productive employment that would be provided by private enterprise. Indeed the event of extinguishing the national debt would provide a memorable and happy occasion that would serve as a moral example to the whole world. When, during his regime, the public debt was in fact paid off, his Secretary of the Treasury, Levi Woodbury boasted that an "unprecedented spectacle is thus presented to the world."[12]

This "unprecedented spectacle" led to another. The man who followed Jackson into the presidency, Martin Van Buren, was the only president to assume office in the absence of public debt. In the early days of his administration the most troublesome problem was once again that created by the existence of surpluses. However, the recession of 1837–1838 led to a sharp drop in customs duties and a sudden deficit. But this cyclically-caused deficit was no occasion for jettisoning the budget balance constraint. As Van Buren put the matter, "the creation in time of peace of a debt likely to become permanent is an evil for which there is no equivalent." Much as Alexander Hamilton had argued, Van Buren was convinced that the credit of the United States would be impaired and any emergency funds would be difficult to raise. He combined this idea with a political argument. The "coffers of foreign stockholders" would give foreign countries too great an influence in domestic affairs, a sentiment later echoed in the fears expressed concerning the possible investment by Arab sheiks of OPEC funds in the United States. But more important was Van Buren's recognition that a weakening of the budget balance rule would tend toward an illegitimate growth of the public sector. Public debt, he argued prophetically, has "its inevitable tendency to increase in magnitude and to foster national extravagance."[13]

Van Buren's admonitions were to be repeated over and again by

12. *Ibid.*, p. 20.
13. *Ibid.*, p. 22.

succeeding presidents. To John Tyler, for example, "a public debt
in time of peace should be sedulously avoided." His Secretary of
the Treasury, George M. Bibb, in lyrical tones, attributed the period
when the federal government was free of debt to "the beneficent
smiles of an all-wise and protecting providence." This attitude
continued under Zachary Taylor whose inaugural address in 1849
promised prompt extinguishment of the debt; and under Franklin
Pierce who proclaimed debt reduction as a cardinal principle in his
philosophy. And it is reassuring that a president with the name of
James Buchanan should have seen public debt as a burden on future
generations. "This disgrace must not fall upon the country," he
warned darkly.

This viewpoint which amounted to constitutional constraint on
the size of the state was augmented by the attitudes of the leading
economists of the era. More than at any other time in our history,
public figures were familiar with the ideas of economists who had a
prestige that today perhaps is only approximated by physicists.
Many of the Founding Fathers were themselves contributors to
moral philosophy of which political economy was a branch.
Doubtless they were familiar with David Hume's dictum that "it
would scarcely be more imprudent to give a prodigal son a credit in
every banker's shop in London, than to empower a statesman to
draw bills in this manner upon posterity .... It must, indeed, be
one of two events; either the nation must destroy public credit, or
public credit will destroy the nation."[14] To Hume's friend and
neighbor, Adam Smith, public expenditures were unproductive and
wasteful. His ideas, which greatly influenced Alexander Hamilton,
were a corollary of his wages fund doctrine. Public debt will
eventually mean higher taxes which must fall on the owners of
capital stock and on agriculture. A higher tax on landlords meant a
decrease in the funds used by them to hire productive workers and
improve the land. That would mean a reduction in agricultural
employment, the most productive of all sectors. Moreover, a tax on
entrepreneurs would mean that less would be available for the
payment of productive workers in industry, a consequent reduction
in the extension of the division of labor, and a fall in productivity
and a decline in real wages.

David Ricardo, whose views were well known to many members

14. David Hume, *Essays on Public Credit* (London, 1752), p. 4.

of Congress,[15] had a position similar to Adam Smith's on the subject of public debt. Ricardo is best known in public finance for the "equivalence theorem" that now bears his name, to wit, that a rational person should be indifferent between the payment of a tax and the issue of public debt of equal value. The individual can always borrow at the same rate as the government and pay his taxes now; or he can purchase government securities and hold them using the interest to pay taxes and simply exchange the matured debt in meeting his tax obligation when it falls due in some future period. The possibility of effecting transactions in the capital market without cost should therefore make an individual indifferent between the two fiscal possibilities.[16] Notwithstanding his belief in the equivalency of the two fiscal instruments, Ricardo opted for taxation to cover all expenses of the state since a fiscal illusion exists that made people prefer debt to taxes. The use of public debt has a tendency "to blind us to our real situation."[17] He recommended that the public debt be paid off immediately through the use of an extraordinary tax or capital levy,[18] and advocated a pay-as-you-go system of public finance.

Other classical writers followed Smith and Ricardo in rejecting deficit financing. Even Malthus, who believed in the efficacy of public works during depressions, was convinced that public expenditures must normally be held within strict limits. He, too, adhered to the wages fund theory. Taxes interfered with the efficient operation of the economy since they reduced capital accumulation and economic growth.

John Stuart Mill, who stated the wages fund theory in its most uncompromising form, was also unable to find a favorable word for

15. Joseph Dorfman has pointed out that half of the first American edition of Ricardo's *Principles of Political Economy and Taxation* was subscribed by government officials. See Joseph Dorfman, *The Economic Mind in American Civilization*, Volume I (New York: The Viking Press, 1946) p. 369.
16. David Ricardo, *On The Principles of Political Economy and Taxation*, edited by Piero Sraffa with the collaboration of M. H. Dobb (Cambridge: At the University Press, 1953) pp. 244–245. For a discussion of Ricardo's theorem, see E. G. West, "Public Debt Burden and Cost Theory" *Economic Inquiry*, Volume XIII, June 1975, pp. 184–187. See also James M. Buchanan, *Cost and Choice* (Chicago: Markham Publishing Co., 1969) pp. 65–67.
17. David Ricardo, *op. cit.*, p. 247.
18. A good discussion of Ricardo's views on the capital levy and debt retirement can be found in R. M. Hartwell's introduction to the Pelican Classics edition of Ricardo's *Principles of Political Economy and Taxation* (Baltimore: Penguin Books Inc., 1971) pp. 26–27.

public debt. Such borrowing came out of funds that would have been channeled into private investment. Ultimately public borrowing came at the expense of the wages of the laboring classes. Thus Robert J. Walker, Secretary of the Treasury under President Polk, was drawing upon the best economic theory of his day when he stated in his "Report on the Finances" in 1848 that "Wages can only be increased in any nation, in the aggregate, by augmenting capital, the fund out of which wages are paid. . . . On the other hand, the deduction or diminution of capital, by destroying or reducing the fund from which labor is paid, must reduce wages."[19] Since public debt reduced the capital fund destined for the payment of wages, it is responsible for a reduction in the demand for labor and lower wages.

It should by now be clear that among political leaders in the first half of the nineteenth century, the budget-balance norm was so deeply ingrained as to form a constraint of considerable power on the actions of government. The second half of that century did not provide a significantly different record in this regard. With the sole exception of Abraham Lincoln under whose administration a large national debt accumulated during the Civil War, a balanced-budget philosophy remained intact. During the second half of the century, cash surpluses existed during times of prosperity and deficits in time of depression. But it was the cyclical rise and fall of revenues that led to the imbalance in accounts, not discretionary countercyclical changes in expenditures and taxes.[20] Indeed any movement away from balance was treated as a source of grave concern. Right up to the first term of Franklin D. Roosevelt this attitude persisted. The words of Roosevelt in a radio address to the nation in July, 1932, could have as well been said by Theodore Roosevelt — or Woodrow Wilson — or Herbert Hoover: "Let us have the courage to stop borrowing to meet continuing deficits. Stop the deficits . . . . Revenues must cover expenditures by one means or another. Any government, like any family, can, for a year, spend a little more than it earns. But you and I know that a continuation of that habit means the poorhouse."[21]

19. Cited in Kimmel. *Op. cit.*, pp. 24–25.
20. John M. Firestone, *Federal Receipts and Expenditures During Business Cycles, 1879–1958* (Princeton: Princeton University Press for the National Bureau of Economic Research, 1960).
21. Cited in Frederick C. Mosher and Orville F. Poland, *The Costs of American Governments* (New York: Dodd, Mead & Co., 1964) p. 73.

By the onset of the Great Depression some economists had begun to question the balanced-budget philosophy, leading to a sharp split in the profession over this topic. In Great Britain the issue was brought to a head in Keynes's battle with what was called "the Treasury View," a doctrine dubbed by T. W. Hutchison "one of the main classical dogmas, of obvious Smithian and Ricardian lineage."[22] The argument of the Treasury was that deficit financing should not be used to combat unemployment. The reasoning shows that the wages fund doctrine, which John Stuart Mill had allegedly "recanted" in 1869, still had its adherents. Government borrowing reduced the stock of capital which would have been used by private enterprise to hire productive workers. In the White Paper of May, 1929, when unemployment was roughly 10% of the labor force, it was firmly stated that: "The large loans involved, if they are not to involve inflation, must draw on existing capital resources. These resources are on the whole utilized at present in varying degrees of active employment and the great bulk is utilized for home industries and commercial purposes. The extent to which any additional employment could be given by altering the direction of investment is therefore strictly limited."[23]

Letters in the *Times* during the early depression years showed the split in the British economics profession most starkly. On one day a letter attacking the Treasury View would appear bearing the signatures of luminaries like Keynes, Pigou, Macgregor and Sir Josiah Stamp. A few days later an attack would follow with a letter bearing the equally distinguished names of von Hayek, Lionel Robbins, Arnold Plant and T. E. Gregory.[24]

22. T. W. Hutchinson, *Economics and Economic Policy in Britain, 1946–1966* (London: George Allen and Unwin, Ltd., 1968) p. 19.
23. Cited in Hutchison, *Ibid.*, pp. 19–20.
24. A letter signed by Keynes among others read in part, "The public interest in present conditions does not point towards private economy; to spend less money than we should like to do is not patriotic . . . . If the citizens of a town wish to build a swimming bath, or a library, or a museum, they will not, by refraining from doing this promote a wider national interest . . . . Through their misdirected goodwill the mounting wave of unemployment will be lefted still higher." *The Times*, October 17, 1932. A reply signed by Hayek and others said in part, "We are of the opinion that many of the troubles of the world at present are due to improvident borrowing and spending on the part of public authorities . . . . The depression has abundantly shown that the existence of a public debt on a large scale imposes frictions and obstacles to readjustment very much greater than the frictions and obstacles imposed by the existence of private debt. Hence we cannot agree with the signatories of the letter that this is a time for new municipal baths, etc., merely because people 'feel they want' such amenities." *The Times*, October 19, 1932. Both letters are cited in Hutchison, *Ibid.*, pp. 19–21.

In the United States a similar bifurcation of opinion can be found. Until the turn of the century American economic thought was single-mindedly opposed to deficit financing. Then some slight relenting in this position can be discerned. Henry Carter Adams, for example, favored a balanced budget but believed that between the choice of a deficit or a surplus, a deficit was to be preferred. The reason was that a deficit serves to warn the legislator that expenditures must be controlled. So the moral effect was deemed desirable. Richard T. Ely, one of the founders of the American Economic Association, saw the role of the state in far more expansive terms than those envisaged by his more orthodox peers. Nevertheless, he advocated the maintenance of a balanced budget in time of peace. On the other hand, Simon N. Patten was a leading exemplar of the view that national debt, under certain conditions, was a national blessing since it could lead to increased production. But he was virtually the lone exception in the mainstream which adhered to the balanced-budget rule as an article of faith.[25] Perhaps it will be most useful to look at the advice economists were giving to Congress after the onset of the Great Depression. For in that period the division of opinion is sharper, indicating what amounted to a paradigmatic crisis.

One of the striking discoveries one makes when searching through the congressional hearings and *Congressional Record* of the period is how few times economists were called upon to testify about anything before the Great Depression. Like morticians and plumbers bad times for others means good times for us. After the 1929 stock market debacle they increasingly can be found participating in congressional investigations, although businessmen and bankers still outnumber them. Then, as now, there is a wide difference not only in the advice offered, but in its quality.

As might be expected, the performance of Irving Fisher was impressive. He saw that attempting to balance the budget was deflationary while the real need at the time was for inflation, or what he called "reflation." Attempting to balance the budget would lead to deflation, thereby increasing the value of the national debt in real terms. He was for budget-balancing, but only after expansionary monetary policy pulled the economy out of the

25. For an account of the views of Adams, Ely and Patten, among others, see Joseph Dorfman, *The Economic Mind in American Civilization*, Volumes IV and V (New York: The Viking Press, 1959).

depression. As he put it in answer to a question by Senator Thomas
of Oklahoma in May, 1932, regarding the sensibleness of debt
retirement and budget balancing:

> I did not mean, really, to refer to balancing the budget. The proper sequence
> is to reflate first and balance the budget afterwards; and even if we now pass
> laws which will balance the budget next year, between now and then we
> ought to reflate. Reflation is the lesson of the hour for everything; for
> balancing the budget as well as other things.[26]

Fisher also recognized that it was best to issue public debt to the
Federal Reserve System so that money creation would accompany
deficit financing. To put Fisher's arguments into more modern
dress, he was saying that a divorce of spending decisions from
taxing decisions was desirable during the depression. Expenditure
expansion should take place until "reflation," that is, growth in
aggregate economic activity, requires once again the recognition of
the need to tie taxing and spending policies so that the
"constitutional" rule of budget balancing will once again serve as a
constraint on choice.

Among others who had a relatively sophisticated view of these
matters and consequently helped weaken the budget-balance rule
was William Trufant Foster. Foster, along with Waddill Catchings,
was an enormously popular writer on economics. Although
Catchings and Foster are usually classified as underconsumptionists,
they demonstrated a keen appreciation of the importance of the
money supply in maintaining aggregate demand. Today they would
doubtless be placed in the "monetarist" camp.[27] Not surprisingly,
Foster was asked to give his views before a Senate inquiry into the
question of unemployment relief. In the course of his testimony,
Foster advocated public works financed through monetized debt
creation. "The objection to increased expenditures for public
works," he said, "on the ground that such expenditures would
unbalance the budget is not a valid objection."[28] But he added a
warning. "The only valid objection to the proposed course of action
is that it might get out of control. But should we be afraid to create

---

26. Irving Fisher, U. S. Congress, Senate, Committee on Banking and Currency, *Hearings,
Restoring and Maintaining the Average Purchasing Power of the Dollar*, 72nd Cong., 1st
Session, 1932, p. 129. The printed record ascribes the remark to Senator Thomas but it is
clear from the context that the words are Fisher's.
27. For a discussion of Catchings and Foster, see Joseph Dorfman, *op. cit.*, pp. 339–352.
28. William Trufant Foster, U. S. Congress, Senate, Committee on Banking and Currency,
Hearings, Unemployment Relief, 72nd Cong., 1st Session, 1932, pp. 55–64.

enough purchasing power to put men back to work, solely for fear of creating too much? There is danger in overreacting, but no physician ever advocated malnutrition solely for fear that a patient who ate enough might possibly eat too much."[29]

Other economists held to the budget-balance rule and refused to accept the new nostrums being offered. Unfortunately the reasons given by most showed little understanding that abandoning the budget-balance rule during a depression will improve fiscal choice. When resources are unemployed, individual choice is distorted under a budget-balance philosophy. Many of the adherents of the mythological balance rule had little or no understanding of the budget as a weapon of fiscal policy. Functional finance was yet to be born. One of the most remarkable statements was that of Professor F. R. Fairchild of Yale University. At hearings of the Finance Committee of the Senate on the Revenue Act of 1932, which was an attempt to balance the budget, Fairchild made one of the strongest statements for budget balancing that can be found during this episode. He urged increased taxation in order to bring expenditures and receipts into alignment. Moreover, his views on the way in which the revenues should be raised should satisfy the most ardent connoisseurs of the antique: "If I could offer criticism of the general spirit of the House bill, it would be to the effect that too much attention has been given to raising this additional needed revenue from the few who are wealthy and well to do, and too little from the mass of the people."[30] It would surely be impossible for an economist at Yale or any other respectable institution of higher learning to say anything like this today. Fairchild's adherence to budget-balancing was predicated on his belief that it would serve as a stimulus to "the business manufacturing interests of the country." Moreover, he expressed the opnion that budget balancing would be met with approval by all "serious thinkers on public problems," and especially would it meet "the favor of those who are students of political economy."[31]

Although Fairchild was a bit reckless in the assertion that a

29. *Ibid.*, p. 64.
30. Fred Rogers Fairchild, U. S. Congress, Senate, Committee on Finance, *Hearings, Revenue Act of 1932*, 72nd Cong., 1st Session, 1932, p. 154.
31. *Ibid.*, p. 153. It should be noted that Fairchild's views may have been slightly biased. He was testifying on behalf of the Manufacturer's Association of Connecticut.
32. U. S. *Congressional Record* 72nd Cong., 1st Session, 1932, 75 Part 11, 11745–11746.

balanced budget would be approved by all serious students of political economy, other such students did in fact agree. For example, on June 1, 1932, sixty-two members of the Johns Hopkins University faculty sent a communication to the Congress urging prompt action in balancing the budget. This was to be accomplished by "vigorous retrenchment in the expenditures of all federal departments and by adequate emergency taxation." Reaching back to classical economic theory for support they classified government expenditures as "unproductive." So obvious was the need for budget balancing during a depression that the argument for it "can hardly need to be stated." But for the obtuse they did so anyway. Budget balance "is the first essential for the re-establishment of confidence and the renewal of enterprise."[32]

Even Sumner Slichter, who is sometimes depicted as an unqualified proponent of deficit financing during the depression and hence a precursor of Keynes, was saying as late as November, 1932, in a speech before the Academy of Political and Social Science, that although a deficit can be valuable in a period of unemployment, nonetheless, "if the deficit is too large and excites too much alarm, its net effect may be deflationary rather than inflationary, because apprehension over fiscal policy of the Government may cause many business enterprises to postpone buying and . . . to avoid commitments." Slichter went on to offer his opinion that the deficit was already too large and "in order to gain the maximum inflationary benefit . . . it is necessary therefore to reduce the deficit."[33]

Even Slichter's opinion is wildly radical when compared to the

---

33. Slichter's paper was printed in the record of the hearings on unemployment relief. U. S. Congress, Senate, Subcommittee of the Committee on Manufactures, *Hearings, Federal Aid for Unemployment Relief*, 72nd Cong., 2nd Session, 1933, p. 134–137. For the conventional wisdom on Slichter's point of view see J. Ronnie Davis, *The New Economics and the Old Economists* (Ames: The Iowa State University Press, 1971) pp. 12, 18–19. Although in many ways an excellent corrective to the strawmanlike treatment of pre-Keynesian economic views on anti-depression policy proposals, Davis's study is somewhat selective in its approach. At least in regard to deficit financing and the conscious advocacy of the budget as an instrument of fiscal policy, I am persuaded that Keynes's work involved a genuine revolution in thinking. Davis is correct, however, in noting that a belief in the efficacy of an activist government to fight the depression seems to have been stronger at the University of Chicago than elsewhere. Moreover, his study is useful in showing that almost no reputable economists were in favor of wage cutting during this period. For the views at the University of Chicago see Harry D. Gideonse, Editor, *Balancing the Budget: Federal Fiscal Policy During Depression* (Chicago: University of Chicago Press, 1933).

balanced budget philosophy of Alvin Johnson, one of the founders of the New School for Social Research. In an article he wrote in 1933 titled "Debt and the Devil," the older view of budget balance as a constitutional constraint is in evidence; "The way of excessive debt is for a state the way to the Devil."[34]

With Keynes's discovery that fiscal policy can be a weapon in the battle against unemployment, the coup de grâce was given to the constitutional limitation on budget deficits that clearly existed at the founding of the Republic and that held the state in thralldom until Keynes. The chief importance of that ethos was that it made individuals perceive that they paid taxes when government spent. That norm was inevitably relaxed with the demise of the wages fund theory which provided the theoretical underpinning for the balanced budget doctrine. But when modern fiscal policy was born out of the Great Depression, democracy's inherent tendency to choose debt over taxes was accentuated. Indeed so strong should be the temptation to engage in borrowing to finance public goods that it is puzzling that taxes would ever be chosen over debt finance.[35] That we observe a mixture of debt and taxes requires some explanation. Professor Buchanan has argued that public debt creation is limited mainly by the sense of contingent liability that such instruments embody. Government bonds involve aggregate liability for the community. If some cannot meet their share then others will have to bear these costs.[36]

But this limiting force on debt creation would seem compelling only if taxes were imposed to amortize and retire the debt. The question still arises, why not issue debt without any tax liability implied? In other words, interest payments on the debt would be financed out of new debt issue and debt retirement would be financed by further debt creation. Under such conditions no

34. Alvin Johnson, "Debt and the Devil," *Yale Review*, Volume XXII, Spring, 1933, pp. 450–464.
35. As James M. Buchanan has argued, the inherent attractiveness of debt financing arises because it allows an individual to meet his liabilities through a wide range of choice. At no net cost the individual can postpone his fiscal obligation. By doing nothing the individual allows the government at one remove to borrow for him at rates lower than those in the private market. On the other hand, if he desires to discharge his obligation immediately under debt finance, he can do so by buying government securities and holding them until debt retirement at which time his accumulated assets would equal the accumulated liabilities. See *Public Finance in Democratic Process* (Chapel Hill: University of North Carolina Press, 1967) pp. 256–266.
36. Buchanan, *Loc. Cit.*

contingent liability need be feared and there would be no inherent limit on debt creation. Perhaps the answer to this paradox is that offered by Professor Lerner in another context, namely, the "Lerner effect." As public debt is issued, and government spends the proceeds, the money supply remains unchanged. But in addition to the same stock of money, the public holds a near-money – a highly liquid asset that it did not possess before the transaction. In this way the unbalanced budget increases society's wealth. The greater is the private wealth in the form of government securities, the greater is the propensity to consume out of current income. But deficit financing beyond some point will so increase aggregate demand that inflation will set in. The inflation acts as an indirect tax on cash balances. Under a regime of functional finance, the rule to follow would be to tax to prevent inflation. If this rule is not followed, the inflation itself acts as a tax. In either case deficit finance will be seen to involve contingent tax liabilites even in the absence of any explicit decision to amortize and retire the debt out of taxes. At one remove, therefore, taxation is linked to deficit financing. Paradoxically, inflationary expectations may be the ultimate limiting device on debt creation.

The unwritten fiscal constitution of the United States that once involved the maxim of the balanced budget was grounded ultimately on moral and economic mythology. This mystique had the result of chaining Leviathan. Those who see in its unleashing a threat to the liberty of the individual must hope for a new moral equivalent to the budget-balance rule.

COMMENTS

Donald F. Gordon

Let me begin this comment by a brief summary statement of what I conceive to be the main arguments of Professor Breit's paper. He shows convincingly that throughout most of United States history the belief in a balanced budget has been part of the unwritten constitution. He relates this doctrine to classical political economy and, in particular, to the puzzling notions going under the names of the wages fund doctrine. This doctrine, he argues, was in fact a piece of "moral and economic mythology", but it had as a very useful if unintended by-product, the starvation of the Leviathan, or a severe limitation on the size of the state.

Keynes and functional finance destroyed the myth with the discovery that "fiscal policy can be a weapon in the battle against unemployment." But this happy discovery in turn had as a by-product the tendency to unbalance budgets in inappropriate circumstances, and this, in turn, leads, or is likely to lead, to chronic inflation.

I find myself in partial or full agreement with virtually everything in this interesting paper, and I thoroughly enjoyed some of the historical vignettes. However, on some points I find the picture somewhat over-drawn and too simple, and I will address my remarks here to a couple of these issues. The first concerns the classical rationale for budget balancing; the second concerns the causal force of Keynesian economics in creating our present concerns.

If I may put it rather strongly, I believe Breit mildly slanders the classical economists and the wages fund doctrine. The latter was more than a piece of economic mythology or we would have to classify a good deal of modern economic analysis similarly. If there ever was something called "the" wages fund doctrine it originated in a rather inadequate capital theory of a one-good economy (Ricardo's corn model) in which the one commodity was both a consumption and an investment good. It was, in other words, very similar to Frank Knight's use of the bush model to illustrate capital theory and to various similar models in the modern abstract growth literature. It may not be very useful because of its abstractions, or more accurately, because it abstracts from some crucial elements such as the durability of capital goods. But I do not think it is helpful to regard it as mythology or to fail to see its similarity, despite differences in presentation, to some contemporary anlaysis.

Whatever its abstractness, its applicability to the balanced budget doctrine was very pointed. It was the firm conviction of the classical economists that governments waste, either by useless as opposed to desirable consumption, or even more, by draining resources from investment into current consumption. A rule of budget balancing will, they further believed, hold down government expenditures, hence increase investment and thus support frugality in its rather unequal contest with population. And it would hardly be an exaggeration to say that this struggle between sex and thrift was the main issue in applied economics for the nineteenth century, and that for the classical economists the outcome of this contest would be the overwhelming determinant of the happiness and welfare of mankind.

While the struggle between sex and thrift may not seem important to us today, it clearly did not disappear as a problem because of the appearance of the *General Theory*. It is equally obvious that the extent to which governments waste resources did not change sharply in 1936. One of the hypothetical and non-operational historical issues in which I like to indulge myself is the question as to whether, if Ricardo and Smith could wander through the halls of the federal triangle today, they would find much to change in their attitudes to government spending. But whether they were correct or incorrect regarding the inherent profligacy of governments, the issue seems to be one of fact, or better, of positive political science or public choice theory; it does not seem to depend upon the wages fund doctrine.

I turn now to the effects of Keynesian economics. Both Breit and the classical economists would agree that access to deficit spending puts more resources at the disposal of governments, and in many circumstances this is undoubtedly correct. Nevertheless I think that the causal chain in Breit's paper has links which are neither necessary logically nor without empirical exceptions. As I understand it, the sequence starts with the theory of employment, which leads to deficits, which lead to enhanced government, which creates inflation.

However the modern growth of government use of resources began long before 1936 and may have continued in much of its present form even without that revolution. It was in 1883 that Adolph Wagner enunciated his law, according to which the development of capitalism and the technical complexities of modern society lead inevitably to a rising absolute and relative level of government spending. Even then he had some empirical evidence, and from then until the 1930s there was a more or less continually rising trend of government expenditures as a fraction of total output in the most important economies of the western world. This was accompanied by no visible weakening in the doctrine of a balanced budget and no significant inflation. Again, since 1946, state and local spending which, despite New York, is much more subject to balanced budget pressures, has risen from about one third to about two thirds of federal spending. Turning to the other side, in South America violent inflations were produced before and therefore without benefit of the *General Theory* or of a large government share of output. Since World War II among the industrialized countries Japan has had one of the highest rates of inflation and one of the lowest proportions of government spending in gross national product. Thus on a rather crude empirical level Keynesian economics and inflation seem to be neither sufficient nor necessary conditions for large government.

On the analytical level, even if one accepted the fiscal policy implications of the *General Theory*, one could argue, as was almost immediately perceived after 1936, for continual tax cuts or even for negative taxes, rather than for feeding the Leviathan. Moreover we can hardly overlook the monetarists. Despite the controversial status of the fiscal- monetarist debate, I suspect that there are few economists who would question the proposition that the central bank could generate, if it had the will, a massive inflationary increase in aggregate demand without touching the doctrine of balanced budgets. It may be that the massive increases in government spending which we have observed would have occurred without Keynesian economics, and the complex reasons for these increases should be, have been, and will be subject to increasingly refined analysis in terms of public choice theory.

It should be noted that while I have argued that large government may be independent of full employment policies and inflation I am not claiming that the latter two are independent. Certainly Keynesian economics is inflationary, but not because it necessarily leads to big government. Fundamentally it is inflationary because it recognized that unemployment can be created by sticky wages as well as by a high marginal disutility of labor. It provided no theoretically satisfactory explanation for such stickiness, but it correctly posited its existence, I believe, for the analysis of cyclical problems. The Phillips curve may be a theoretical monstrosity but it does summarize a short-run set of facts. As a consequence, increases in normal demand can almost anytime set "idle" resources to work, whether or not the increased demand stems from rising government spending, reduced taxes, or increases in the money supply.

While such policies are ultimately inflationary the political contest between anti-inflationary and anti-unemployment policies has been heavily weighted in favor of inflation. I remember reading some years back a discussion by Professor Lerner on the merits of suppressing a three percent inflation at the cost of three percent more unemployment. During the past couple of years Keynesian economists have called for massive stimulus in economies experiencing year to year rates of inflation of ten to twenty percent. On the analytic and scholarly level the anti-inflationists have been very weak. Even now I do not find in the scholarly literature any convincing cost-benefit case for more unemployment now and less inflation in the future, and this perhaps illustrates Keynes' hypothesis concerning the ultimate power of academic ideas, or in this case the helplessness of a position without academic theoretical and empirical support. The proverbial "average intelligent layman" would, I suspect, be appalled at what he would consider the triviality of the nature and magnitude of what academics discuss as the costs of inflation. In any case Keynesian economics may ultimately create big government by saddling us with permanent wage and price control.

E. G. West

I shall preface my comments by a brief digression on Alexander Hamilton. Whilst Professor Breit is undoubtedly correct that Hamilton was a careful reader of Adam Smith's *Wealth of Nations* we must avoid the danger of over-association of the two. Hamilton after all was a mercantilist, being a supporter of legislation that favored the American manufacturing interests. One of his reasons for wanting to re-establish confidence in public loans was his desire to pave the way for a strong federal government that was to base its numerous economic activities on federal debt. Nothing could be further from the spirit of Adam Smith — as my final observations will demonstrate.

Beyond this initial digression, my main comments will attempt to extend William Breit's interesting survey of the classical economic literature on balanced budgets, although this might involve some slight points of debate between us. I take my cue from his remarks that, "so strong should be the temptation to engage in borrowing to finance public goods that it is puzzling that taxes would *ever* be chosen over debt finance." Professor Breit draws on James Buchanan's argument that there is an inherent attractiveness of debt financing because it allows an individual to meet his liabilities through a wider range of choice. The individual can postpone his fiscal obligation at no net cost. He allows the government at one remove to borrow for him at rates lower than those in the private market. If he does not want to borrow and to take this advantage, the option is still open to him to discharge his obligation immediately by buying government securities and holding them until such a time as he has to pay his contribution to debt retirement. It needs to be emphasized, I think, that Buchanan's argument is based on very special assumptions that he himself eventually relaxes. But more on that later. For the moment I want to concentrate on what I believe to be the origins of this idea of a comparative cost advantage in publicly negotiated loans.

Notice first that this same proposition that the government has an advantage in borrowing in the capital market is basically in opposition to Ricardo's famous equivalence theorem. Ricardo's theorem states that there is *no* difference between an individual paying his whole share of the government project straight away in a lump sum tax payment, and the alternative of public borrowing with taxpayers subsequently paying back in installments. If the public sector can get access to loans at cheaper rates than in the private capital market, then there *is* a difference; and Ricardo's equivalence theorem is challenged.

The idea of favorable borrowing terms in the public sector can be traced to the classical economist J. R. McCulloch. In his book *Taxation and the Funding System*, published in 1845, McCulloch openly challenges Ricardo on the subject.

> When government goes into the money-market and contracts for a loan, it borrows, no doubt, for those who would otherwise have to borrow for themselves; but it does not negotiate a separate loan on account of each indiviudal; it borrows for them in a mass, and pledges the national credit in security for the entire loan. By this means the loans for the behalf of those whose security is comparatively indifferent, are obtained on the best terms, and the total payment for interest is considerably less than it would have been had a series of loans been contracted by private parties. In this respect, therefore, the system of funding is preferable to the plan for raising the supplies within the year.[1]

If such access to borrowing at a favorable public rate of interest is available, and provided the individual knows with certainty the pattern of his income receipts and his private spending over the

1. *Ibid.*, pp. 421–422.

relevant planning period, it would seem that he would always choose that *all* public goods and services be financed through public debt issue. Today, however, we are prompted to search for the fallacy that lurks in all this. One aspect of the fallacy became known at the University of Virginia as "Tullock's Fallacy"[2] after Gordon Tullock. This relates to the proposition that one should always prefer debt to taxes. This proposition seems independent of the possibility of government obtaining superior terms. McCulloch's Fallacy, in contrast, depends entirely on the argument that government has a cost advantage. Before we look closer for the real "fallacy" in McCulloch's proposition, I believe I can express it in even more striking terms. If specially favorable terms on the capital market are obtainable by government there is no reason why *private* goods as well as public goods cannot be financed on the same principle; I refer especially to private consumer durables that are normally purchased in installments (hire purchase). Government should provide borrowers of all kinds, and for all purposes, in the private as well as in the public sector if indeed all the welfare conditions are to be fully met.

To get now to the heart of the McCulloch fallacy; we have first to focus upon its assumptions. The fact is that they are profoundly unrealistic. James Buchanan has formally demonstrated this in his book *Public Finance in Democratic Process*. I shall show later however that, at least in one sense, it was Ricardo who got there first with such criticism. As Buchanan reminds us, it is unrealistic to assume that the individual knows with certainty his income prospects and his private spending plans over the relevant time span. Because of uncertainty the individual does not know whether in the final accounting period, when debt must be retired, he will be rich or poor. But even if the individual is fully certain of his own future income prospects he will not be informed of those of his neighbors. If others fail to live up to their rationally projected plans, their plight will impose a *contingent liability* on our selected individual. But this means that because the individual faces the probability distribution of default among his neighbors, the real price, or shadow price, facing him for loans provided through government has to be increased or "grossed up." It is then no longer obvious

2. J. M. Buchanan, *Public Finance in Democratic Process* (Chapel Hill: University of North Carolina Press, 1967), p. 257.

that an individual *can* borrow at preferable rates through government; and the McCulloch Fallacy is exposed.

Although McCulloch chided Ricardo for not having seen what he
thought to be the economic virtues of public debt usage, he did not
read the master with sufficient care. Ricardo was sensitive to the
fact that the income of different individuals can fluctuate over
time. Such fluctuation occurs either because of accidental reasons,
such as the unexpected changes in market demands for people's
services; or because of deliberate behavior by individuals in
attempting to avoid their responsibilities by reducing their income
and therefore their tax liabilities. It was this latter behavioral
response, that now goes under the name of "moral hazard," that
Ricardo was at special pains to expose. When a country had
accumulated a large debt, Ricardo observed:

> It becomes the interest of every contributor to withdraw his shoulder from
> the burthen, and to shift this payment from himself to another; and the
> temptation to remove himself and his capital to another country, where he
> will be exempted from such burthens, becomes at last irresistible, and
> overcomes the natural reluctance which every man feels to quit the place of
> his birth, and the scene of his early associations.[3]

It was for this reason indeed among others that Ricardo himself did
not really "believe in" the "Ricardian equivalence theorem." It was
one of those Ricardian abstractions that even Ricardo did not want
to dwell on.

Consider next William Breit's provocative observation that "When
fiscal policy was born out of the Great Depression, democracy's
inherent tendency to choose debt over taxes was accentuated." We
should surely pause to ask why the tendency was "inherent."
Assistance comes to us now via the new discipline of the economics
of politics. If we assume that the self-interest of politicians
manifests itself in the short term pursuit of optimal voting support,
the bias in favor of public debt can easily be predicted. In Anthony
Downs' celebrated work[4] governments and politicians are posited
to have an interest in maintaining ignorance among voters and in
obfuscating the issues. Insofar as this is true public debt provides
the very kind of "fiscal illusion" that such politicians and
governments require. The use of debt makes it more difficult to

3. David Ricardo, *Principles of Political Economy and Taxation* (Pelican Classic, 1971), p. 255.
4. Anthony Downs, *An Economic Theory of Democracy* (New York: Harper, 1957).

identify the ultimate bearer of its burden. Moreover since the Downsian theory postulates that politicians are more sensitive to the interests of *median* voters, and especially if these voters are more sophisticated than others in the knowledge of their own interests, it will pay politicians and governments to shift the debt burden marginally upon the shoulders of the lower income groups. This may well have been the basic reason for the opposition to public debt of President Andrew Jackson of which William Breit reminds us. Jackson protested that the servicing of the debt with interest payments came from customs duties and other regressive taxes. If we assume that citizens receive benefits from public projects that are proportional to their income, then the appropriate taxes, on equity grounds, are proportional taxes. If public debts are serviced in practice by regressive taxes as Andrew Jackson believed, the explanation could be that politicians are indeed favoring the critical median voters whilst deluding others.

The choice of public debt meanwhile would also seem to be in accord with the economic objectives of bureaucrats. It is arguable that bureaucrats who are motivated primarily from concern for the size of their budgets can fare better on public debt than on annual taxes, first because their budgets can sometimes escape the necessity of annual votes; second because public debt affords more opportunities for increasing the coefficient of ignorance among taxpayers and others. Ricardo was one of the first to argue that public debt can blind us in this way:

> From what I have said, it must not be inferred that I consider the system of borrowing as the best calculated to defray the extraordinary expenses of the State. It is a system which tends to make us less thrifty − to blind us to our real situation.

The equivalence theorem of Ricardo collapses, therefore, for this additional reason: there is no equivalent impact on thrift between debt and taxation. And here Ricardo was echoing the sentiments of Adam Smith. The incentives to go to war, financed by public debt, Smith emphasized, were *not* equivalent to the incentives when the war was financed by direct taxation. In Śmith's words,

> Were the expense of war to be defrayed always by a revenue raised within the year, the taxes from which that extraordinary revenue was drawn would last no longer than the war. ... Wars would in general be more speedily concluded, and less wantonly undertaken.[5]

Smith was aware that economic decisions are made against the background of positive information costs; and such costs vary according to the institutions of public finance adopted. Insofar as we are interested in voters as decision-makers, the "arithmetic" of calculation they perform under a system of public debt will produce different answers to those derived under a system of direct taxation. This was the essence of the original Smithian message which has seemingly taken 200 years in the delivery.

The concept of fiscal illusion relates to all the hidden costs in institutions of public finance – in our case the institution of public debt. One of the major remaining costs to be considered is inflation, inflation, that is, as a form of hidden taxation. William Breit attributes the modern recognition of this to Professor Lerner. Adam Smith however was, I believe, the first to begin to expose it; and in no uncertain way. Indeed Smith described it in stronger terms than "inflation"; to him it was public *bankruptcy*. In this bicentenary year of *The Wealth of Nations* it is fitting for me to end my comments with one more relevant quotation from that great work:

> When national debts have once been accumulated to a certain degree, there is scarce, I believe, a single instance of their having been fairly and completely paid. The liberation of the public revenue, if it has ever been brought about at all, has always been brought about by a bankruptcy. . . . The raising of the denomination of the coin has been the most usual expedient by which a real public bankruptcy has been disguised under the appearance of a pretended payment. . . . A national debt (our present one) of £218 millions might in this manner be paid with about £64 millions of our present money. It would indeed be a pretended payment only, and the creditors of the public would really be defrauded of ten shillings in the pound. . . . It occasions a general and most pernicious subversion of the fortunes of private people; enriching in most cases the idle and profuse debtor at the expense of the industrious and frugal creditor. . . . The honor of a state is surely very poorly provided for, when, in order to cover the disgrace of a real bankruptcy, it has recourse to a juggling trick of this kind. . . . .[6]

---

5. Adam Smith, *The Wealth of Nations* (Cannan Edition: Methuen, 1950), Vol. II, p. 411.
6. *Ibid.*, p. 415.

3. THE DECLINE OF THE BUDGET-BALANCING DOCTRINE
or

HOW THE GOOD GUYS FINALLY LOST

Herbert Stein

I hope it is understood that the title of this paper, part of which was assigned to me and part of which I chose, is not to be taken seriously. The title implies that there was a budget-balancing doctrine in 1929, when my story begins, that this doctrine subsequently declined, and that this decline was a defeat for the good guys. I am not sure that any of these propositions is true. However, I want to discuss them and also the question of how the change of attitude towards budget-balancing, to use the more neutral term rather than decline, happened.

Initially one should distinguish between at least two possible meanings of the budget-balancing doctrine. One is the idea that the budget should be continuously balanced, or at least balanced in every fiscal year. The other is the idea that the budget should be balanced over a longer, unspecified, period, with the deficits of some years being balanced by the surpluses of other years. Later we shall have occasion to refer to somewhat more complicated meanings of budget-balancing, such as balancing at full employment.

We should also distinguish, where we can, among four different meanings of the idea that the doctrine exists:

1. That the doctrine is followed in practice;
2. That public officials believe in the doctrine;
3. That economists believe in the doctrine;
4. That the public believes in the doctrine.

Surely, annual budget-balancing was not the practice of the Federal government, even before 1929. In the 140 years of the nation's history from 1789 to 1929 there were 47 years of budget deficit, about one-third of the total. There were always deficits in war years, including the years of minor wars — the Mexican War and the Spanish-American War. (Although we managed to fight the Battle of Little Big Horn without a budget deficit.) We also generally ran deficits in years of depression, or right after. The depression of 1873 was an exception, but the budget did go from a surplus of almost $100 million in 1872 to a surplus of only $2 million in 1874.

Whether our pre-1929 practice should be considered one of balancing the budget in the long run depends on how literally one interprets balance. The Federal government, which started with a Revolutionary War debt and incurred some more in the War of 1812 repaid it all, except for about $37,000, by 1834. However, this result was at least in part accidental. We had that lovely protective tariff, which was not imposed for revenue but which yielded a large amount of revenue nonetheless. Since the Federal government had no Budget Bureau it didn't know what to do with all that money and so used it to repay the debt.

After the Civil War there was a run of 28 years of consecutive budget surpluses — surely as much as one can reasonably expect — and the debt was reduced from about $2¾ billion to about $1 billion. This was a big cut, but it still left the debt about ten times as large as it had been before the War.

In eleven consecutive years of surplus after World War I the debt was reduced from about $25½ billion to about $16 billion, which was still fourteen times as large as the pre-war debt. Whether this experience reflects a fierce determination to eliminate the debt is hard to say. From today's standpoint the achievement of the budget surplus in the 1920s seems easy. We were having our first important peace-time experience with that marvellously elastic revenue producer, the income tax, individual and corporate. Expenditure programs had not yet adapted to the fact that in a period of prosperity and economic growth this tax would yield strongly increasing revenues. That is, they did not build in expenditure increases to absorb the growing revenues. So surpluses came easily. Some of these surpluses were given away in tax reductions. However, the revenues frequently exceeded the estimates so that unplanned surpluses emerged. Secretary of the Treasury Mellon claimed that the increased revenues were the result of the tax reductions. However, he was cautious about testing this theory further by making bigger tax cuts.

All of these numbers about the size of the debt up to 1929 look small to us today, and there is a temptation to say that for all practical purposes the debts were eliminated after the Civil War and World War I. But that would not be quite accurate. In 1894, when the Civil War debt reached its low point it was still three times a year's Federal revenues and the interest was about 10 percent of the total revenues. In 1929 the Federal debt was about four times a year's revenues, and the interest on the debt was about 17 percent of the revenue. By these standards it seems an exaggeration to say that the pre-1929 practice was to eliminate the wartime deficits in peacetime.

Perhaps a more relevant standard is the relation of the Federal debt to the GNP. Of course, measurements of the GNP for earlier periods are pretty rough, but the Federal debt in 1894 was probably about 7½ percent of the GNP. In 1929 the ratio was about 16 percent. These are not insignificant fractions.

In summary, budget-balancing in the years before 1929 meant in operation that there would be deficits in wars and depressions, which would be followed by surpluses that reduced the debt absolutely and relative to the GNP, but that did not reduce it to zero. The long-run trend of the debt was up, absolutely and relative to GNP. Whether one should say that the United States practiced budget-balancing is a matter of taste.

The opinions of responsible Federal officials about budget-balancing in the pre-1929 period are unclear. During World War I the Secretary of the Treasury and other officials were quite concerned with the inflationary consequences of excessive reliance on debt financing, and their discussion of the question in general terms seems fairly modern. What was most lacking was any notion of the relevant quantities. The Administration therefore made the predictable decision to finance the war half by borrowing and half by taxation. In actuality the part financed by borrowing was more than half.

After the War, during the 1920s, officials made frequent reference to the desirability of balancing the budget, but without ever revealing what they meant by it or why they thought the budget should be balanced. As far as I can see, they were not then concerned with possible inflationary consequences of deficits. About the most that can be inferred from the statements of Presidents Harding and Coolidge is that the debt should be reduced in order to reduce the interest payable, directly by reducing the principal amount and indirectly by reducing the interest rate through reduction of the outstanding volume of debt. This reduction of the interest burden was desired as a necessary condition for getting taxes down. But why this year's taxpayers should forego tax reduction in order to run a surplus which would allow future taxpayers to enjoy tax reduction was never discussed.

As the unbroken string of surpluses continued through the 1920s, devotion to the idea of balancing the budget each year became more religious, and the reason for that devotion more obscure. In 1922 President Harding faced the prospect of a budget deficit with equanimity, in view of the probability of a surplus in the next year. (Actually the prospective deficit did not materialize.) By 1929 the Director of the Bureau of the Budget was giving the Federal officials an inspirational talk about saving money to keep the string of surpluses going like a Big Ten Coach who needed one more win to go to the Rose Bowl.

However, the practice of budget-balancing in the 1920s was child's play, as I have already explained. The real test of meaning and will was to be faced by Herbert Hoover, when revenues fell off in the recession and demands for expenditures to provide employment and relief mounted.

At first President Hoover accepted his deficits as the natural and necessary consequences of the depression. Although he resisted what he regarded as extreme spending proposals, he initiated some expenditure increases himself and certainly made no great effort to balance the budget. In his budget message of December, 1930 he said that he did not view with great concern the deficit for the current fiscal year, noting that we could confidently look forward to the restoration of surpluses with the general recovery of the economic situation.

In September 1931 President Hoover turned very actively towards budget-balancing and recommended a large tax increase to achieve it. In my opinion this did not result from any dogmatic devotion of Hoover to a doctrine that the budget should be balanced at all times. He concluded that he was hemmed in by a particular set of circumstances which made a desperate attempt to balance the budget or at least reduce the deficit, imperative. The British went off gold and there was fear that the United States would be next. Interest rates were rising sharply. Banks were dropping like flies. The President felt the need to demonstrate to the world, especially to the financial community at home and abroad, that the dollar was sound and that our credit markets would not continue to be depressed by enormous additions to the Federal debt.

Most of what Hoover was worried about can be summed up in the word "confidence." The need to bolster someone else's confidence is often used as a cover for one's own prejudices and faint-heartedness. It is hard argument to counter because the confidence or lack of it is always difficult to measure and the point cannot be dismissed a priori.

However, it must be said for Hoover that the hard facts of the situation were pretty bad. For one thing, he had to deal with an especially uncooperative Fedral Reserve. I treasure as an example the following note of George L. Harrison from a meeting of the Federal Reserve Bank of New York on January 7, 1932: "If we are to deviate from straight and narrow central bank theory because of the terrible economic situation, the government must do all it can to improve the situation − we require an authoritative pronounce-ment of its intentions with respect to borrowing between now and July 1 and a commitment to operate on a balanced budget beginning July 1, 1932."

As I shall mention below, economists generally considered to be more sophisticated and modern than Hoover saw reasons why the conventional acceptance of depression deficits might not be appropriate in 1932.

The general pre-New Deal view of government officials about budget-balancing was that deficits were acceptable in wars and depressions, that the wartime deficits should be limited because of their inflationary consequences and that the debts accumulated in wars and depressions should be subsequently repaid. The reason for the repayment was apparently the desire to reduce future tax burdens. This gave no clue to the desirable pace of debt reduction, and it did not imply a need to run a surplus or even balance the budget every year, or in every year of peace and prosperity.

I will now turn to the doctrine of budget-balancing as held by economists before 1929 or 1932. Two things immediately strike a modern reader surveying economic literature of the 1920s on budget-balancing. One is that the literature is so slight and the other is that there is such a wide gulf between general economics and the discussion of business cycles, unemployment, etc., where the question of budget-balancing comes up in its modern context. Either the economists of the 1920s were much less infatuated with budget-balancing that we later came to believe they had been or they took its virtue so much for granted that they did not feel the need to argue about it.

I take as an example the economics textbook that I used in high school. It was a good little book, prepared under the editorial supervision of Allyn A. Young, Professor of Economics at Harvard. The subject of public deficits or debts comes up only once, in a listing of the various sources of revenues, as is completely covered by the following paragraph:

"Sale of bonds and treasury notes. This is a temporary method of raising revenue; such loans must be repaid."[1]

Another sample of 1920s thinking is a college text, *Public Finance*, by Jens P. Jensen. This book identifies three occasions for public borrowing. One is occasional random errors in estimating or planning the relation of revenues to expenditures. A second is the financing of captial improvements. A third is emergenices, mainly war, but also including earthquakes, foods and epidemics. Depressions are not mentioned. The repeated lesson of the book is to borrow as little as possible and repay it as soon as possible. The apparent reason for this is to preserve the government's credit.

Jensen's text of 1924 should not be dismissed as of antiquarian interest only. It did say: "The enormous debt of New York City, for example, is eloquent testimony to the danger from too much borrowing."[2]

I do not find in the American writing of the 1920s the classic argument that deficits are to be avoided because they absorb private savings and so cut the rate of economic growth. During the debate of 1917 on war finance Senator Stone made this point, and quoted John Stuart Mill in support of it. Perhaps this argument was assumed by American economists. If so, it is worth noting that the

1. Eugene B. Riley, *Economics for Secondary Schools* (Boston: Houghton Mifflin, 1924), p. 259.
2. Jens P. Jensen, *Problem of Public Finance* (New York: Thomas Y. Crowell, 1924), p. 471.

argument does not say anything about whether there should be deficits at any particular time. It is logically only an argument against a deficit in a current accounts budget, from which capital investments have been excluded. And it is a valid argument only to the extent that priority is to be given to economic growth.

Neither do I find in the American discussion of this period any reference to the related argument which was then known in England as the Treasury view. This was the view that government spending financed from borrowing could not stimulate output and employment because the government borrowing would crowd out an equal amount of private spending. It took our Treasury 50 years to acquire the British Treasury view.

In fact it is unclear who did hold the British Treasury view. Keynes in 1929 attributed that view to Winston Churchill, who was Chancellor of the Exchequer. However, he misquoted Churchill, who did not say that it was his view. At the same time Keynes insisted that no leading economist of the United Kingdom would endorse that view. Presumably it was the property of Treasury bureaucrats.

Probably this argument did not go on here in the 1920s as it did in Britain because we did not then have a depression as Britain did. But there was in the United States a group of people concerned with planning to deal with a future unemployment problem — having been stimulated by the 1919 depression. They believed that increased public works expenditures financed by borrowing would be helpful, particularly if the borrowing "was assumed by America."

As soon as the issue became an immediate one, with the coming of the Depression, there were large numbers of economists who believed that deficit finance was both inevitable and desirable. Without having taken any poll, I would say that was the standard view among economists.

However, even among economists who took this position there were some who in 1932 were hesitant about the feasibility of expansionary deficit finance, given the international and domestic monetary situation and the state of confidence. I think of Jacob Viner and J. M. Clark in this connection. Viner did suggest that Hoover had created his own problem by insisting that a balanced budget was essential to the national credit until a psychology was created in which it was true. That was probably a little unfair to the President.

In sum, the state of thinking of American economists about budget-balancing at the beginning of the Depression can probably be best described as undeveloped. It was for budget-balancing, but it also recognized a number of real, important conditions in which deficits would be appropriate. It did not rule out deficits in depressions and was ready, when confronted with the problem, to assert the desirability of deficits in such circumstances. Its argument for budget-balancing was an argument for balancing the budget in the long run. But even this argument was not very forceful. It was less a demonstration that a balanced budget is optimum than an expression of fear of the lengths to which the government and the people would go if relieved of the belief that a balanced budget is the normal, natural and necessary state of affairs.

I will not try to describe public opinion, as distinguished from the opinion of government officials and economists, about budget-balancing in this period. There are no polls and I have no other data. Politicians clearly thought then, as they do now, that there was a considerable body of public opinion out there in favor of the balanced budget.

My principal observation from this is that the commitment to the balanced budget, before, say, 1932, was not very great, either in practice or in thought.

How have things changed since? In some respects, or at a certain level of generality, not much.

As far as practice is concerned, we have continued to have a variable budget position, with bigger deficits in some years and smaller ones or surpluses in other years. The biggest deficits come in big wars, and smaller deficits come in smaller wars or in recessions. After the big wars, World War II for our generation, the debt has been sharply reduced relative to the national income.

But in other respects there have been changes. The variations in the size of the deficit or surplus associated with fluctuations in economic conditions have been greater, whether measured in relation to the size of the budget or in relation to the size of the GNP. Although these variations continue to be mainly the result of the automatic response of revenues and expenditures to the change in economic conditions, the automatic responses have been increasingly supplemented by discretionary changes. Also, these discretionary changes have increasingly come on the revenue side of the budget, rather than on the expenditure side.

The main change in performance of the past generation, as compared with the earlier periods, is that the average level around which surpluses and deficits revolved has been a deficit, rather than a surplus. This means simply that after the Civil War for about thirty years the debt was reduced and after World War I for about ten years the debt was reduced, but after World War II the debt was increased.

Despite this difference in the behavior of the absolute size of the debt, the reduction of the debt relative to the GNP has been comparable to that in earlier periods. The Federal (i.e., Union) debt after the Civil War was probably about 50 percent of the GNP. At its low in 1894 it was about 7½ percent. At the end of World War I the Federal debt was about 30 percent of the GNP. By 1929 it had been reduced to 16 percent. At the end of World War II the Federal debt was over 100 percent of the GNP. It is now about 30 percent.

While the debt is now larger relative to the GNP than it was on the earlier occasions, it is much smaller relative to the Federal revenues. Even after the deficit forecast for fiscal 1977 the debt would be about 1.6 times the year's revenues, as compared with three times in 1894 and four times in 1929. Interest on the Federal debt would be about 10 percent of the revenues, the same as in 1894 and less than in 1929.

Now it is true that a large part of the reduction of the ratio of the debt to the GNP has been due to inflation. If there had been no inflation after 1946, and the debt had followed its actual course, the ratio of debt to GNP would have fallen from 100 percent to 75 percent, rather than to 30 percent. Whether the fact that the debt was rising in absolute size, even though less rapidly that real output, caused or contributed to the inflation is an interesting question which I assume to be beyond my present assignment.

The inflation may not have reduced the interest burden on the debt, because the inflation tended to raise interest rates.

This difference of performance, the increase of the debt after World War II contrasted with the decrease in its absolute size after the Civil War, does not necessarily reflect doctrinal differences. The circumstances since 1946 were in some respects more difficult than in the earlier period. We did have two wars after 1946, whereas the periods 1865 to 1894 and 1918 to 1929, when the debt was being reduced, were years of peace. Even when we were not at war we had a heavier military burden than in the earlier periods. Also, we have had more serious recessions than during the 1920s, although not worse than in the 1870s.

So, even if there had been the same determination to reduce the debt absolutely as in the earlier periods less might have been accomplished because the obstacles were greater. However, the fact is that there was less determination. One evidence of this is that there was no provision after World War II, as there was after World War I, to set up a sinking fund and make annual reduction of the debt a regular charge against the budget.

The cumulative deficits of the post-World War II period through 1975 have been around 1 percent of GNP. To have kept the absolute size of the debt from rising would have required that on the average surpluses should be larger and deficits smaller by 1 percent of GNP. The swings from surplus to deficit between peace and war or between prosperity and recession could have been of the same magnitude as they were. But everything would have gone on at a higher level of surplus or smaller level of deficit. This would not, I think, have made stabilization policy any more difficult, or the management of war finance any more inconvenient. It would not have been impossible. But it would have required a willingness to pay more taxes relative to the expenditures, and this would in turn have required a belief that over the long run avoidance of absolute increase in the debt was highly valuable. This belief has not been present.

The change in the view of the budget problem held by public officials in the past 40 or 50 years is pretty obvious, despite their periodic regression to the language of more innocent days. Whereas they had always, or almost always, accepted the fact that they would have deficits in depressions, they now came to accept much larger deficits, relative to the GNP or to the budget. Moreover, they came to accept the notion that they should take active steps which would increase the deficit in recessions and that the proper size of these steps was the size needed to get the economy back to where it should be in the short run. It was a short-run econometric problem.

That is, they became true believers or camp followers of functional finance, of the view that the proper deficit or surplus is the one that gets the economy onto its optimum feasible path. Presidents have been uneasy with this position, which left the debt at the mercy of the economy and the economists, and they have sought some more reliable or familiar anchor. Thus Roosevelt toyed with the idea of balancing the budget over the cycle, or with balancing a current-accounts budget. When Truman proposed a deficit during the 1949 recession he consoled himself and the country by explaining that the budget would return to balance at full employment. Eisenhower, Kennedy and Nixon each at times described his policy in terms of balancing the budget at full employment. But this was mainly salve for their own consciences or for what they believed to be the public conscience. It did not much deter them from doing what they thought was in the short-run economic interest and within the limits of political feasibility.

A policy of functional finance does not necessarily mean that the deficit cumulates over long periods. It only says that we should have the size of deficit or surplus at any time that will get us on the optimum feasible path. Whether this policy leads to deficits or surpluses in the long run will depend on how the optimum feasible path is defined, how the economy behaves spontaneously in relation to the path, and how other policies which might affect the behavior of the economy, such as monetary policy, are managed. The fact that functional finance has yielded a long-run deficit during the postwar period does not mean that Alvin Hansen was finally right and that we have entered the age of secular stagnation. It may mean that we have defined the optimum state of the economy too exclusively in terms of the unemployment rate, and of too ambitious an unemployment rate, so that inflation accelerates and the needed deficit increases. This is probably part of the explanation for the tendency of functional finance to lead to long-run deficits in the postwar period.

Another aspect of functional finance needs to be mentioned in this connection. To conduct a policy of functional finance requires estimates of the size of the surplus or deficit needed to get on the optimum path. But the President's economists cannot tell him within a wide margin what that proper size is. Within that range he has to make that choice himself, and he is not neutral about where he makes it. If his economists cannot tell him that a $10 billion deficit is better than a $20 billion, he is likely to choose the $20 billion, because the voters like tax cuts and expenditure increases. This bias is increased when the Congress enters the picture.

From time to time the classic argument against deficits on the ground that they absorb saving and slow down economic growth has surfaced in official thinking. President Eisenhower used this point in recommending a budget surplus in 1960. We have been hearing it again recently from Washington, especially from the Secretary of the Treasury. However, I believe that Eisenhower's push to balance the budget was primarily motivated by shorter-run considerations — fear of inflation and worry about our balance of payments.

The meaning of the current interest in "crowding out" is unclear. It could mean that beyond some size a deficit is undesirable because it makes the economy rise too fast and is inflationary. Alternatively it could mean that beyond some size a deficit is excessive because it undesirably restrains private investment, even though it does not cause an excessive rise of aggregate demand. Or it could mean that beyond some size a deficit is contractionary, because its restrictive effect on private investment outweighs whatever stimulative effects it may have.

I find the third view, that a larger deficit is contractionary, hard to credit, although it sometimes seems that it is what is being said and it is always possible to get any results one wants if one is free to choose assumptions about confidence and psychology. The second interpretation seems to me a more logical possibility, but it would involve the government in saying that it wants to slow aggregate expansion below its optimum rate in order to get private investment up to its optimum rate. I don't think the government is saying this. I think that for the present it is only saying that too big a deficit would be too inflationary. They may be trying to stake out some claim for a budget surplus in the future to speed up growth, but that is to happen only when it is possible, presumably meaning when the ordinary canons of functional finance would call for a surplus anyway. There is no explanation of how that condition is to be brought about in the future if it so rarely occurred in the past thirty years.

In sum, official attitudes to budget-balancing now ignore the size of the debt, the burden of the interest charges and the long-run size of the deficit. We are all functional-financers now, concerned to find the best size of this year's deficit for this year's economic conditions. President Ford may feel more of a twinge of pain at an $80 billion deficit than, say, Senator Humphrey does, but that is not the reason for a difference in their policy. The reason is that President Ford thinks that in the particular economic circumstances of 1976 a deficit of that size is more inflationary than Senator Humphrey thinks it is, and that President Ford thinks inflation is more damaging than Senator Humphrey does.

There is probably little reason to discuss the doctrines of economists about budget-balancing separately from the views of public officials. There is little difference between the views of the officials and the predominant views of the economists. Many of the politicians are economists and even more of the economists are politicians.

However, I will attempt some classification of the opinions of economists. This shows considerable difference of opinion. However, it shows little support for the idea that there is a presumption in favor of balancing the budget, over either long or short periods. It seems to me that the following schools can be distinguished:

1. *The pure, old-fashioned Keynesian functional financers.* They believe there is a direct, unique connection between the deficit or surplus and the state of economy, so that if you know the desirable state of the economy you know the desirable size of the deficit or surplus, aside from difficulties of estimation. That is the size of the deficit or surplus you should have. The cumulative deficit or surplus will be the sum of these short-period deficits and surpluses, and should be; there is no other test of the desirable long-run behavior of the deficit or surplus.

2. *The fiscal-monetarists.* They deny that fiscal policy has any direct effect on aggregate demand, which is governed by monetary policy. However, they believe that monetary policy is governed by fiscal policy, in such a way that if there is a big deficit there will be rapid monetary expansion. Therefore, there is always one and only one size of deficit or surplus which will yield the right rate of monetary expansion to yield the right rate of rise of aggregate demand. They wind up in the same place as the old-fashioned functional financers.

3. *The monetarist-Parkinsonians.* They believe that the behavior of aggregate demand is determined by monetary policy and unaffected by fiscal policy. Also there is a political law which says that the government will spend all its tax revenues, over a reasonably short period, and will not spend more, so there is no realistic question about deficits or surpluses. The object of

policy is to hold the size of government down, which can best be accomplished by holding down taxes.

4. *The monetarist neutrals.* They also believe that the behavior of aggregate demand is determined by monetary policy. The size of the deficit or surplus in the long run affects the rate of economic growth, through the effect on the supply of saving available for private investment. However, what is the desirable rate of growth is not a question that economists can answer for the society, given that growth is not free. The size of the surplus or deficit has to be decided in the political process, and there is no presumption that the answer will be or should be a surplus.

5. *The supply-side fiscalists.* They also believe that aggregate demand is determined by money. However, aggregate supply is determined by taxation, including negative taxation, or transfer payments. Both inflation and unemployment can be reduced by reducing taxes and transfer payments, and that should be the objective of policy. It may be implied that surpluses are better than deficits, but probably only because they are the route to tax reduction.

6. *Conventional eclectics.* They believe that both fiscal policy and monetary policy affect aggregate demand. Therefore, the optimum behavior of aggregate demand can be achieved by any one of many combinations of fiscal and monetary policy. However, since they have not yet figured out how to put these combinations into their models they continue to operate as old-fashioned, one-dimensional, functional financers.

7. *Growth-oriented eclectics.* These believe in the possibility of different fiscal-monetary mixes to achieve specified behavior of aggregate demand. They also believe that more rapid economic growth is desirable. Therefore, they recommend a policy with long-run budget surpluses, and whatever complementary monetary policy is needed to get high employment. However, the time to get on this policy is later, not yet.

As far as I can see, none of these schools implies any presumption for budget-balancing, in the short run or in the long, except for the last, which has not yet been tested in the crucible of any specific decision.

I will turn now from the opinions of officials and economists to the opinions of the general public on the subject of budget-balancing. For as long as we have had public opinion polls, that is, for a little more than forty years, about 70 percent of respondents to such polls have given answers which showed some belief in balancing the budget. We have no direct evidence from polls on how deeply they felt about that. However, we do know that they went on voting for Presidents and Congressmen who produced deficits, so I would conclude that they did not feel very deeply about it and did not rank devotion to budget-balancing very high among the criteria by which they judged public officials.

Something more may be said about the views of one sector of the public, the business community, partly because its views are more elaborated in print and partly because I have myself had more direct contact with it than with other sectors.

The businessman is traditionally the fiscal conservative and defender of the balanced budget. In the 1930s, in the early days of the New Deal, the utterances of business organizations and business leaders were thick with complaints about the Administration's failure to balance the budget. However, my reading of that literature convinces me that they really didn't care much about that, and only emphasized it to put themselves in line with a feeling which they thought was widespread in the country and against the Roosevelt Administration. What they really cared about was keeping down taxes, especially on business, and fending off government regulation.

One rather sad evidence of this came after the recession of 1937. Treasury Secretary Morgenthau tried to convince Roosevelt that the way to get recovery would be to restore the confidence of the business community by promising it a balanced budget, and Roosevelt was briefly tempted by the idea. Morgenthau then went to talk to a group of businessmen and made a speech about balancing the budget which he thought would evoke warm support. Instead he got a cold reception, he was discouraged, and Roosevelt turned in the other direction.

I had my own experience on this subject in 1947 when I worked for the Committee for Economic Development and we were writing the policy statement that recommended the policy of balancing the budget at high employment. This statement was intended to be about tax reform and we got into the question of budget policy only as a way of determining how much revenue we had to raise. We made some estimate of the minimum necessary expenditures and quickly decided that the revenues should be sufficient to yield a surplus of "X" at high employment. We then faced the question of how high "X" should be. It was recognized that although there might be some level of "X" that would be inconsistent with the achievement of high employment, nevertheless there was a range within which we could choose. The higher "X" was, the larger the surplus would be, or the smaller the deficit, in the long run. Also, the higher "X" was, the higher the level of taxation would have to be. The Committee's decision was dominated by the desire to keep taxes, including business taxes, low. Therefore they chose as small an "X" as they thought would look respectable.

I think it is also of some interest that in the recent furor about the capital shortage, it is not the business-people who are plumping for budget surpluses as a solution. That is the route chosen by economists, and "liberal" economists at that. The preferred route of the business community is tax reduction, especially reduction of taxes on capital. This difference is perfectly natural, because the issue is not only, or mainly, how much capital formation there should be but who should own it and what the return on it should be.

My conclusion is that there is nobody out there who cares very much about balancing the budget. There wasn't a strong belief in this as a primary objective of national policy in the 1920s, and there is less now. How did this change occur?

The change in practice and doctrine is the result of a long list of developments in the real world and in theory since 1929, which I will put down here in no particular order:

1. Hoover was inhibited about continuing to run deficits by the uncooperativeness of the Federal Reserve about financing enough of the deficits to keep interest rates from rising. The Federal Reserve has since been more cooperative.

2. Hoover was also inhibited by fear of the response of foreign holders of dollars to the sight of our budget deficits. For a great variety of reasons we have become much less worried about what foreigners think of the dollar.

3. We had willy-nilly, by the sequence of Great Depression and Great War, a long string of large deficits and woke up to discover that none of the bad consequences which were predicted had come about, or at least that they could not confidently be pinned on the deficit. This was extremely damaging to the popular prejudice against deficits. There was even a belief that the deficits of the 1930s had contributed greatly to the recovery from the Depression, which was at least debatable but became part of the mythology nonetheless.

4. There was the Keynesian Revolution, which converted a generation of economists and other intellectuals to the belief in the efficacy and harmlessness of deficit finance.

5. The big increase in the size of the Federal budget relative to the GNP automatically increased the size of the fluctuations of the surplus or deficit relative to the GNP. It accustomed us to bigger deficit figures.

6. The change in the composition of the Federal revenues and expenditures made them more elastic with relation to the GNP and so increased the variability of the deficits and surpluses and made the task of keeping the budget in balance much more difficult.

7. The huge absolute size of the debt at the end of World War II, instead of making the need to reduce it seem great made the possibility of any significant absolute reduction seem remote.

8. At the same time, at the end of World War II, we were becoming acquainted with the figures about the rate of national growth, and impressed with the prospect of being floated off the real burden of the debt by rising GNP. It seems to me that belief in the high probability of rapid growth is important in explaining willingness to assume and maintain large debts. Essentially the classical argument works in reverse. Why should I pay taxes to reduce the debt so that private investment can exceed private saving, accelerating economic growth and making my grandchildren richer than I am, when it is likely that they are going to be richer than I am anyway? At

the end of 1974 the Federal debt was 21 times as high as at the
end of 1929. At the end of 1974 private consumers' credit was
27 times as high as at the end of 1929. The same attitude that
we are going to be richer later may help to explain both
phenomena.

9. Perhaps this is saying the same thing, but the claimants on
   government programs also became used to the growth of the
   economy and of the revenues, and programs were shaped to
   absorb the revenues. There was no growth dividend to which a
   vigorous claim had not been asserted and which could be
   painlessly applied to reduction of the debt.

10. The business community, which might have been the claimant
    for debt reduction, was staggered by the tax burden it faced
    and was not inclined to put debt reduction ahead of tax
    reduction.

11. Our whole generation was saddened and frightened by the
    experience with unemployment in the Great Depression and so
    became extremely sensitive to the need for supportive, and
    deficit-creating, action by the Federal government when faced
    with a rise of unemployment.

12. Whatever mystique there was once about the budget-balancing
    rule, and there was some, it could not be transferred to a new,
    more realistic rule devised by human hands and not handed
    down from Mount Sinai. We discovered that in the CED with
    respect to the rule of balancing the budget with a moderate
    surplus at high employment. Even the Committee that wrote
    the rule was not prepared to be disciplined by it, perhaps
    because they knew that its origins were not divine. The rule
    involves a number of arbitrary decisions. How much is high
    employment? How much is a moderate surplus? Which of the
    possible definitions of the budget is to be used? If provision is
    made for exceptions, how are the exceptions to be identified?
    How are we to estimate what the revenues and expenditures
    would be under conditions we have never experienced, and
    how would we ever know if the estimates had been correct?
    Now it is possible to show that the same or similar arbitrary

arbitrariness is involved in the old-fashioned budget-balancing rule. But that only serves further to demystify the old rule. It does not transfer any mystique to the new one.

I seem to have come out to the same point as I did in my book. The revolution was not really revolutionary. It was a change. The good old days before the change were not so great. The bad new days after the change are not so terrible. We are feeling unhappy because we have discovered that we really don't know enough to manage the economy as well as we would like. But we never did. We can't go back to the old myths and wouldn't like it if we did. And we can't create new myths, at least not consciously by holding conferences for that purpose. The only way out of our present predicament is to try to go forward and learn more, not to try to go backward and unlearn what we have learned.

COMMENTS

Armen A. Alchian

First I want to strongly endorse the remarks of Donald Gordon who anticipated much of what I had proposed to say. So instead I turn to some side remarks about a basic theme of the conference and a romantic point of view about government that is, in my opinion, dangerously naive for scholars of the world as it is.

The conception of Government Fiscal Responsibility reminds me of the myth of corporate social responsibility. Neither exists. Responsibility suggests an obligation or duty to behave in some prescribed way. Or it can mean bearing the consequences of one's actions. Or it could mean responsiveness to the desires of the governed. None are descriptive of actual political behavior. You may argue the politician is responsive to the will of the people. That is, of course, a vacuous nonrefutable statement — like the music of our national anthem.

What is government? It is the ultimate repository or controller of the power of physical force — the military. That monopoly is the necessary and sufficient condition to be a government. A temptation to interpret government as a social contract agreed to by the populace reflects our own idiosyncratic origins of the United States.

Generalizing from so special and rare an event is romantic, not scientific. Political philosophers enjoy that sport. But why should economists, who presume to be scientists, not moralists?

Some economists talk about budget balancing as if it were some standard for government behavior. Some of us talk about failure of the government — political power — to respond to the public will. Some talk about the government being out of control or that the budget is growing out of control. I do not understand any of that. I don't know what is meant by responding to public will, or to the desires or beliefs of people on issues of which there are conflicting interests.

As Mencken said before me, I find watching a political convention is like watching gangsters selecting their leader who will then extort and steal your wealth. From that point of view what does *government* fiscal responsibility and a balanced budget mean?

Let me illustrate with a not so far-fetched example. The Mafia (if it exists) in Sicily is an unrecognized government. But it is acknowledged as existing. Suppose you were called as an economic advisor to the Mafia. Would you say, "Balance your budget"? What would that mean? Would you tell a thief, a successful one, to balance his budget — by spending less, by thieving more, or by earning more in conventional ways? If the Mafia can extort funds or tax people how does that differ from taxes or inflation? Does the Mafia contribute to aiding some of the poor? It does. Does it preserve peace in the area? It does. Are its extortions different from some taxes and expenditures by diplomatically recognized governments? I think not in any significant manner.

A conception of government as solely a sort of agent of the public, a sort of impersonalization of representation of each of us (rather than also as a vehicle for some to achieve benefits) doesn't fit my perspective. We should, I believe, analyze, as some of you are, how individuals who are more adept in the competition to acquire political power do compete for it, and how uses of that political power differ under different modes of competition for acquiring it, such as by elections (with what kind of franchised electorate?), hereditary succession, military succession, or whatever means of classifying access to government power might be appropriate.

Whether the Keynesian doctrine and advice was influential to a degree worth attention in affecting government policy is impossible to refute. Even without any such doctrine, I believe government expenditures, financing and activity would not have been significantly different. In looking at the past few millenium I find little that is different today in government tax, money and spending activity. Nor do I see any significant difference in its regulatory activity. (Consequently while Stein may prefer to believe that Keynesian economics as a belief or doctrine may have been influential, I am unable to do so. I am not sure from his paper whether he believes that.) We easily find doctrines to justify what it is in our interest to do — a doctrine superficially divorced from our own interests. Like the Prince, we hear what we want to hear.

Colin D. Campbell

The historical development of the concept of the high-employment budget and the graduate shift in fiscal rules (from an annually balanced budget to a budget balanced at high employment) are important parts of the fiscal revolution discussed in this paper by Herbert Stein and described in greater detail in his excellent book, *The Fiscal Revolution in America.*[1] The high-employment budget is a measure of the effect of budget policy as distinguished from the response of the actual budget to fluctuations in economic activity. By those who favor a fiscal rule over discretionary changes in fiscal policy, it is now generally agreed that the rule to be followed ought to be to balance the high-employment budget rather than the actual budget.

Not all economists are in favor of fiscal rules. There are many who advocate compensatory or functional finance. Stein has concluded both in this paper and in his book that the advocates of compensatory finance have won the battle. He states that "We are all functional-financers now." It seems to me that this conclusion may be premature. On the basis of his own writing, Stein himself would not be included among those who advocate functional finance. There are other influential economists who doubt that discretionary countercyclical stabilization policy can achieve its goals.[2]

1. Chicago: University of Chicago Press, 1969.
2. For a recent analysis of the difficulty of administering functional finance, see William Poole, "Reflections on U. S. Macroeconomic Policy," *Brookings Papers on Economic Activity* 1 (1974), pp. 233–246.

One way to evalute the role of budget-balancing is to look at the statistical data on the high-employment budget. Table 1 shows the data for the high-employment budget for calendar years 1968 through 1976, as published by the Federal Reserve Bank of St. Louis.

Table 1. Federal Government High-employment Budget, 1968-76 (billions of dollars)

Calendar Year	Receipts	Expenditures	Surplus or deficit (−)
1968	$174.4	$180.9	−$ 6.4
1969	201.2	188.8	12.5
1970	211.9	203.4	8.5
1971	218.4	218.7	− 0.3
1972	236.5	243.1	− 6.7
1973	268.9	264.0	4.9
1974	311.9	298.2	13.7
1975	334.6	347.7	− 13.1
1976 (estimate)	373.4	382.7	− 9.3

Source: Federal Reserve Bank of St. Louis, *Federal Budget Trends* (Feb. 18, 1976).

What do the statistical data on the high-employment budget from 1968 to 1976 tell us about fiscal responsibility (the subject of this conference) or about the decline in the budget-balancing doctrine (the topic of Stein's paper)? Has fiscal policy been irresponsible? Has there been a decline in budget-balancing? The data on the high-employment budget do not give much support to the belief that budget policy has been reckless. In each year, deficits have been small relative to the levels of expenditures or tax revenues. Although both taxes and expenditures have risen sharply, they have risen together. Expenditures have not been increased without the taxes necessary to pay for them. Statistical data on the unified budget, particularly during the past few years would show a different picture. However, changes in the high-employment budget are probably a better indicator of the responsibility of fiscal policy than changes in the unified budget. In recent years, for example, federal government policy-makers have pursued an anti-inflationary policy which unavoidably resulted in a recession and large deficits in the unified budget. Since the principal goal of a responsible fiscal policy is usually considered to be the avoidance of inflation, it would appear unjustified to conclude that the recent deficits in the unified budget were evidence of fiscal irresponsibility.

The statistical data on the high-employment budget for the past nine years also show that receipts and expenditures have been kept close to balancing. It is doubtful that the balancing of the high-employment budget is just a matter of change or that it occurred even though it was unintended. Although Stein's summary of what people say about budget-balancing is undoubtedly correct, what people do is more important than what they say. There appears to be some adherence to the principle of budget-balancing.

Although the high-employment budget has not been far out of balance during the period from 1968 to 1976, there is also evidence of compensatory finance. The data on the high-employment budget show that fiscal policy was tightened in 1969 and 1973; the budget moved from a deficit to a surplus. This probably reflects efforts by policy-makers to combat an acceleration in the rate of inflation. After the recessions of 1969-70 and 1973-75, fiscal policy was eased; the budget moved from a surplus to a deficit. Even though there has been some fine tuning, the changes in the deficit or surplus have been moderate.

Despite the fact that the high-employment budget has been kept close to balancing, inflation has accelerated and reached much higher levels than is customary. Blame for the inflation probably ought to be attributed to monetary policy rather than to fiscal policy (from 1962 to 1973 the rate of increase in the money supply steadily accelerated). Of course, fiscal and monetary policy are interrelated. Economists at the Federal Reserve Bank of St. Louis believe that the more rapid rate of expansion in the federal debt since the mid-1960s (as a result of more expansionary fiscal policies) underlies the accelerated expansion of the money supply (1975 appears to be an exception).[3] However, monetary policy is not dependent solely on fiscal policy. Federal Reserve authorities have been concerned primarily with stabilizing interest rates and have let the rate of expansion in the money supply become too high. Also, monetary policy has overreacted to both unemployment and inflation, resulting in unstable and excessive rates of expansion in the stock of money.

Finally, fiscal policy may be compared with monetary policy

3. Darryl R. Francis, "How and Why Fiscal Actions Matter to a Monetarist," *Federal Reserve Bank of St. Louis Review*, May 1974.

from the point of view of having rules to guide policy. The role of rules in the operation of fiscal policy is probably greater than the role of rules in the operation of monetary policy, even though the use of fiscal-policy rules receives little general endorsement. Among those who favor a rule for fiscal policy, there is at least agreement that the rule should be to balance the high-employment budget. Such a consensus is lacking in monetary policy. Some economists recommend stabilizing interest rates; others recommend stabilizing the rate of expansion of the money supply. This disagreement is a major problem for current monetary policy.[4] Also, the use of wide discretion is probably easier in administering monetary policy than it is in administering fiscal policy because of the cumbersome nature of fiscal policy. A major impediment to the development of functional finance is the difficulty in carrying out such a policy. Given the gap between actual and potential output, it is not easy to fill the gap by manipulating taxes and federal expenditures. As a result, fiscal policy tends to be relatively stable compared to monetary policy. If fiscal policy is compared with monetary policy, the outlook for the role of rules in the administration of fiscal policy appears to be more favorable than Stein thinks it is.

4. For a discussion of this issue, see A. James Meigs, *Money Matters* (New York: Harper and Row, 1972), Ch. 18.

4. KEYNESIANISM: ALIVE, IF NOT SO WELL, AT FORTY

Abba P. Lerner

Keynesianism is the *new way of thinking* about the economy which John Maynard Keynes promised to provide in his *General Theory of Employment, Interest and Money.* It was, of course, not a new kind of logic or some way of thinking "with ones blood" or anything like the mystical irrationalisms with which we are plagued today. Any genuine contribution can consist only of pointing out logical errors, of spelling out implicit assumptions or of changing the assumptions. Of these three, the first disqualifies the conclusions and the second opens up the theory to scrutiny, but only the third can lead to different conclusions. If the different conclusions suggest different policies to be followed, the contribution can be important in determining what those in authority should be not only *thinking* but *doing* about the economy. This is what Keynes had in mind when he bragged about what he was going to do, and I do not see how anyone can doubt that he did indeed succeed in doing this. The essence of the Keynesian revolution was to establish the recognition of the *responsibility of the government* to maintain a satisfactory level of employment in the economy — by showing that there is no effective automatic market mechanism for achieving this.

The recognition of this responsibility is frequently denied even by those in the government who are actively engaged in carrying it out. Thus, we have our President, as well as almost all the candidates opposing him, declaring their loyalty to the principle that the government budget ought to be balanced, but nevertheless planning or demanding large deficits as necessary for adequate employment.

Keynes also contributed in the two first ways. He pointed out errors of applying micro-arguments to macro-issues, such as taking Mr. Micawber's excellent advice for David Copperfield's private budget, and applying it to the budget of a sovereign nation, or crudely generalizing an individual employer's ability to vanquish his competitors and hire more workers, if he could cut the wage he pays, to arrive at the conclusion that a general wage cut would increase *general* employment. He also spelled out the implicit assumptions which underlie the Classical Economists' conclusion that there *is* a satisfactory automatic full-employment mechanism. But there has been a confusion between these contributions and the much more important one of establishing governmental responsibility for an adequate employment policy.

One result of this confusion was a reversal of the normal response by the old guard to any revolutionary idea. The normal response goes from "what strange nonsense" to "that's what we always said − or at least what we meant to say." But in this case the same formulas, instead of being used to claim that they had always held the new doctrine, were used to *misinterpret Keynes* so as to be able to claim him as a supporter of the old doctrine (in a more up to date model − improved by his clarifications of the implicit assumptions). Those who reject this claim are charged with the heresy of "Keynesianism" of which John Maynard Keynes himself is absolved.

As a consequence I am frequently asked by eager students, in hushed tones and with raised eyebrows, whether it is really true that I am still a "Keynesian." This bothers me and other Keynesians and this is what could make Keynes feel not so well.

But it is not a serious sickness. It is only a minor unpleasantness in the realm of theoretical disputations in the history of economic thought. In the world of practical policy, the basic Keynesian principle − governmental responsibility for an acceptable level of employment − is very much alive and flourishing. This is what must be credited for the unprecedented government budget deficits (for peacetime), thanks to which we are being spared the much more serious depressions that otherwise would be upon us. The more vigorous high-employment policy that would be possible is, however, in part held back by the aid and comfort which the shanghai-ing of Keynes gives to the crude micro-to-macro economic generalizations that are so natural to the businessman.

The situation reminds me of Mark Twain's report, in his "letters from the Earth," of Adam's first great contribution to science. He refers not to the Adam whose book is now enjoying its bicentenial, but to the Adam of Adam and Eve, and tells of how he discovered the Principle of Fluidic Precipitation — the law that water flows downhill, not up; and how the discovery of the law later got into dispute and the credit was given to a more recent person. Keynes' principle of governmental responsibility seems to be about as firmly accepted as Adam's law. I sometimes wonder whether it will have to be rediscovered all over again by a "more recent person" before it will be applied in full force.

To clarify these perhaps cryptic remarks, I will consider four steps in the development of the Neo-Classical Model. It was apparently built on, or at least constructed in response to, a part of the Keynesian analysis. First is a "crude Keynesianism" of the introductory chapters in macro-economic text books. It explains the level of income as determined by the investment and the propensity to save (alias the multiplier).

This is not Keynes' "General Theory" (which, we should remember, he called the general theory of *Employment, Interest, and Money*). It is a simplification of the General Theory that leaves out money. It was put forward by Keynes only for the special case of a deep depression when providing more money would not help. But so admirably did it fit the depression of the 1930s that it stuck in the minds of many who forgot the rest of the General Theory. Or perhaps they never learned it. As my mother used to say: "If you never knew, and you forgot, it is very hard to remember." Sometimes the term "Keynesians" refers to those who got stuck at this stage.

The second step brings in the supply and demand for money in the form of an LM curve to complement the IS curve implied in stage 1. Equilibrium now requires that for any combination of income and interest levels, not only must desired saving (S) be equal to actual saving and a desired investment (I) equal to actual investment (and thus $I = S$, since actual I and actual S are always equal), but the desired stock of money (L) must be equal to the actual stock (M) supplied by the authorities.

At this stage the model could properly be considered a synthesis of parts of the Keynesian and parts of the classical analysis. It is not really Keynesian since it says nothing about full employment or about governmental responsibility for it. It is certainly not classical since it is compatible with any level of involuntary unemployment and says nothing about full employment or about any automatic mechanism for achieving it.

The third step consists of repeating the classical declaration that unemployment will cause wages to fall, and that this will restore full employment. It also, incidentally, rehabilitates the classical conditions of full employment: equality of the wage to the marginal disutility of work and equality of the wage to the marginal (value) product of labor.

Keynes called these the two classical axioms. He rejected the first because his "General Theory" included less-than-full employment, and unemployed workers looking for work have a marginal disutility of work which is *less* than the marginal utility to them of the wage. But he failed to reject the second axiom, although it too applies only in full employment. Less than full employment occurs only in a depression when employers would love to employ more workers if only they found the extra customers to buy the extra product. It would increase their profits. But it would do so only if the marginal (value) product is *greater* than the wage.

At this stage the model is perfectly classical. But it does not show how the fall in wages would restore full employment. In fact the argument looks very much like the individual employer's crude generalization to the economy as a whole about wage cuts in his factory.

The fourth step, which completes the neo-classical model, consists of filling in the assumptions under which the fall in wages would indeed bring about full employment. The missing assumptions were provided by Keynes – or perhaps they were always there, implicit in what the classical economists "always meant to say." As spelled out they are as follows: Wages and prices and money income will fall, while the quantity of money does not fall (or at least falls less) until prices have fallen far enough to make the real value of the money stock great enough to make the rate of interest low enough to make the investment big enough to raise consumption and income high enough to result in full employment. In Keynes' words "it is therefore on the effect of a falling wage – and price-level on the demand for money that those who believe in the self-adjusting quality of the economic system must rest the weight of their argument; though I am not aware that they have done so."[1] And "If, indeed, labor were . . . to reduce its money demand . . . to whatever point was required to make money so abundant relatively to the wage-unit that the rate of interest would fall to a level compatible full employment, we should, in effect, have monetary management by the Trade Unions, aimed at full employment, instead of by the banking system."[2]

The explicit recognition of the necessity of these assumptions and their general acceptance is what led to the widespread announcements of a few years ago that "we are all Keynesians now" and to the Neo-Classical Model being billed as a Neo-Classical *synthesis* of Keynes and the Classics.

This leaves us with a puzzle. The "Neo-Classical Synthesis," with its assumptions as spelled out by Keynes, shows how flexibility of wages leads to full employment. Only an *inflexibility* would prevent the automatic mechanism from bringing about full employment. Why then did Keynes repeatedly insist that inflexibility downward of wages (and consequently of prices) was *not* the issue and why did he persistently assert that flexible wages would make depressions worse rather than better?

The answer to the puzzle is to be found in distinguishing between two different meanings of "flexibility." The flexibility required for the Neo-Classical model is an *ideal* flexibility that Keynes considered of no relevance for any problem of the real world. The spelling out of the implicit assumptions was undertaken by Keynes only in order to show up the ideal and impractical nature of the implied inflexibility, and all the more effectively to *reject* the assumptions and to dismiss any reliance on that kind of flexibility. Indeed he did not even find it possible to take it seriously. This is shown — though apparently not clearly enough — in the language he used when he tried to envisage its operation. He had to assume some non-existing institution like the "monetary management by the Trade Unions" in the quotation above from page 267, or to declare explicitly that "the assumption (of the maintenance of income in the face of a shift in "the demand for capital" or "the amounts saved out of given income) could only be saved by a *complicated assumption providing for an automatic change in the*

1. John Maynard Keynes, *The General Theory of Employment, Interest, and Money* (New York: Harcourt, Brace, 1936), p. 266.
2. *Ibid.*, p. 267.

wage-unit of an amount just sufficient in its effects on the liquidity preference to establish a rate of interest which would just offset the supposed shift, so as to leave output at the same level as before."[3] And even when, for the sake of an argument, he did assume ideal flexibility, he did not see it leading to full employment. Thus when he says "if . . . money wages were to fall without limit whenever there was a tendency for less than full employment . . . there would be no resting place below full employment," he does not pause at "full employment" even to put a comma, but continues with "until either the rate of interest was incapable of falling further or wages were zero,"[4] in the course of an argument on the necessity of some price rigidity for monetary stability.

The flexibility that Keynes objected to was not the unrealistic *ideal* flexibility implied or assumed in the neo-classical model. It was another kind of flexibility altogether. It was the *practical* degree of wage flexibility one could reasonably expect to be achieved by governmental policy. This kind of flexibility would be slow and uneven, with *falling* prices and expectations of further price reduction. It would only postpone spending and intensify the depression; and the policy would be abandoned long before prices were *low* enough and the value of the money stock big enough to start the movement towards full employment.

What I am saying here appears to many as a denigration of Keynes. I am in fact declaring that there is no new theory at all in the General Theory. Rather than finding the classical theory wrong, Keynes only fixed it up by filling in the tacit (or missing) assumptions. What kind of revolution is that? Not even any broken eggs for the omelet!

The answer is that it was a *practical* revolution – not a revolution in economic theory. It was more like the English than the Russian Revolution, killing fewer people and keeping the Royal Family with limited functions. The classical economists, just like Keynes, held that if wages did not fall, unemployment would not be automatically cured. The revolution was in thinking *what to do* – in the judgment that trying to create the ideal flexibility is impractical and that government action is required to increase *demand at the current prices*.

This makes many theoretical economists unhappy. Teaching

3. *Ibid.*, pp. 179–180, emphasis supplied.
4. *Ibid.*, p. 303.

economics consists so much of correcting logical errors that a fixation on logic becomes an occupational hazard. It leads economists to expect, nay to demand, some *logical* innovation in any respectable revolution. Because of this there has developed an active sport, among admirers of Keynes, of seeking out truly original theoretical contributions in the "General Theory" to lend authenticity to the Keynesian revolution. And among these Keynes himself was not missing. The hunt has turned up a number of unconvincing candidates for the prize for theoretical originality. Among these are: expectations in economic decisions, the demand for cash balances, the liquidity trap, the centrality of uncertainty in investment decisions, the equality of saving and investment, the propensity to consume and the multiplier. Occasionally incidental asides are offered, such as the euthanasia of the rentier, the desirability of more socialization of investment and the dangers of false liquidity creation and of destabilizing speculation on the stock exchange.

And then there are over-enthusiastic Keynesians − perhaps I should rather say over-enthusiastic anti-classicals − who are not satisfied with merely noting the non-existence of the foundations on which both the classical and the neo-classical edifices stand. They waste their energies in attacking the impregnable logic of the super-structure. This leads them to such exercises as denying the tautologies of Say's Law and Walras's Law; playing with fixed coefficients of production so as to escape contamination with marginal analysis (supposed guilty of improper and indefensible moral implication or of the improper philosophical sins of assuming perfect knowledge and perfectly competitive equilibrium); exaggerating the uncertainties of life, the vagaries of group psychosis and the flexibility of the monetary and market mechanism, so as to throw out the baby of rational public *policy for full employment* together with the dirty bath-water of the foundationless *automatic full employment*; declaring that all economics has been rendered obsolete by joint stock companies becoming multi-national corporations; or even outlawing all attempts at rational thought, by demanding that "everything be taken into account − dialectically."

At the same time a different game is being enjoyed by those who feel that Keynes had been given too big a hand. In attempts to solve the problem by denying the facts, some declare that the "involuntarily unemployed" are really employed in searching for better jobs, or that the unemployed are only supplying the demand for customers by the welfare- and unemployment compensation-industries. Others question the comparability of our statistics with those of countries with far lower unemployment figures. Some, mistaking symptoms of unemployment for causes, take employers' requests for diplomas (so as to reduce the crush of job applicants) as showing a genuine need for unavailable skills, while others cloud the issues by developing unusual terminologies for Keynes' concepts. Thus, Leijonhufvud elaborates an analysis of "quantity responses" (rather than price responses) to disequilibrium. I take this to mean that inadequate demand results in depression and unemployment instead of price and wage deflation, while Clower explains depression as due to "constrained demand" (because of reduced income) – a new name for depression.

Perhaps the "most unkindest cut of all" is the development, in Keynes' own Cambridge, of a "post-Keynesian" school which, in ideological or political revulsion against marginal analysis, finds in Keynes a (perhaps posthumous) intent quite different from both the Neo-Classical doctrine and "pre-post-Keynes" views like my own. Postulating that consumption (C) is approximately equal to the wage bill (W), they find that investment (I, the other component of the income created) must be approximately equal to profits (P, the other component of the income received). They then claim that this equation (I = P) tells us that the share of profits in income is determined by how much the capitalists decide to invest – as if the equations can not be read backwards to read that the level of investment is determined by the share of profits in income, or as if investment has no effect on consumption (C, which = W), or vice versa.

To these disturbances that tend to reduce respect for, and the influence of, the Keynesian Revolution, must be added a number of slips made by Keynes himself in the course of clarifying his thought while writing the book. One slip, mentioned above, was to retain the second classical axiom of the equality of the wage to the marginal (value) product of labor, which is required only for full-employment equilibrium. He also joined the fruitless hunt for a theoretically more exciting basis for the Revolution than the absence of ideal flexibility and the perverseness of practical flexibility. This led to an excursion (ch. 17) into "the essential properties of interest and money" where he makes the "own rate of interest" stand for the marginal efficiency (or rate of return) of *lending* an asset, for the marginal efficiency of *holding* it, as well as for the marginal efficiency of *producing* it. This results in a tangle worthy of Keynes' own sarcasm as displayed in his picture of Hayek as Ibsen's wild duck (p. 183) and in the crushing quotation which shows Hansen confusing the marginal efficiency of investment with the rate of interest in the course of warning his readers against this very confusion. (p. 193)

Another contribution to Keynes' current low Neilson rating is a quality that it is rather rash of me to pronounce. I refer to Keynes' timidity. He did not carry his conclusions all the way. I first was hit by this quality – to my great astonishment – when, at a lecture to the Federal Reserve in Washington in 1944, he showed concern that there might be "too much saving" after the war. When I pointed out that the government could always induce enough spending by incurring deficits to increase incomes, he at first objected that this would only cause "even more saving" and then denounced as "humbug" my suggestion that the deficits required to induce enough total spending could always be financed by increasing the national debt. (I must add here that Evsey Domar, at my side, whispered "He ought to read the *General Theory*" and that a month later Keynes withdrew his denunciation).

In Washington, where he was engaged in difficult international economic negotiations, Keynes was unquestionably overworked and tired. But in the *General Theory* the same timidity shows itself in his comparison of the Neo-Classical with his own recipe for increasing the real value of the money stock. Thus "just as a moderate increase in the quantity of money may exert an inadequate influence over the long term rate of interest, while an immoderate increase may offset its other advantages by its disturbing effect on confidence; so a moderate reduction in money wages may prove inadequate, while an immoderate reduction might shatter confidence even if it were practical."[5] The "Pigou effect," hewing unmercifully to the neo-classical logic, showed how a sufficient reduction in prices must bring about enough spending for full employment, but this is, of course, just as applicable to a sufficient increase in the quantity of money. But perhaps the "moderation" is not really timidity but a practical adjustment to

5. *Ibid.*, pp. 266–267.

the general public's allergy to logical extremes.

By far the most important source of the decline in respectability of Keynesianism is the emergence of "stagflation." This is not, as the name suggests, a kind of inflation — it is a kind of *stagnation*. Prices are rising but this is not due to excess demand being pumped in to inflate the economy — in the way gas is pumped in to inflate a balloon. What we have is a growth of the wage-unit; and in terms of the wage-unit any general rise of prices and wages is invisible. The wage unit — the money wage rate — rises together with the prices. To be applied to our present situation Keynes' analysis must be adjusted, or rather *translated*, from the *wage-unit standard* to the *money standard*.

It is not that Keynes was unaware of the importance of changes in the wage-unit. He spells this out very clearly. "Thus we can cometimes consider our ultimate independent variables as consisting of (1) the three fundamental psychological variables... (2) the wage-unit as determined by bargains reached between employers and employees and (3) the quantity of money..."[6] In speaking of the mercantilists he declares (perhaps over-generously, but that is another story) that "there was wisdom in their intensive preoccupation with keeping down the rate of interest... by maintaining the domestic stock of money and by discouraging rises in the wage-unit; and in their readiness in the last resort to restore the stock of money by devaluation if it had become plainly deficient through a rise in the wage-unit or any other cause." And he adds the footnote: "Experience... indicates... that there is a steady tendency for the wage-unit to rise and that it can be reduced only admidst a decay and dissolution of economic society... thus... a gradually increasing stock of money has proved imperative."[7] Yet when addressing current issues he naturally (in 1935) did not seem concerned about escalation of the wage-unit. "In the long run... we are still left with a choice between a policy of allowing prices to fall slowly with the progress of technique and equipment whilst keeping wages stable, or of allowing wages to rise slowly whilst keeping prices stable."[8]

This option does not seem to be available now. We have not been successful in preventing the wage-unit from rising faster than

---

6. *Ibid.*, pp. 246–247.
7. *Ibid.*, p. 340.
8. *Ibid.*, p. 271.

"economic progress" – the increase in output per man. As we use up our planet we may indeed be approaching a period of "economic regress" with *diminishing* output per man.

In our present situation an important Keynesian policy lesson that seemed to have been absorbed by almost all economists – that the quantity of money should not be reduced in a depression – is apparently being "unlearned." This policy lesson, properly understood, must be read in the wage-unit language. It is the reduction of the quantity of money, and consequently the accompanying reduction of spending and of income, in *wage-units*, that results in the reduction of the wage-bill in wage-units – which means a reduction of "labor-units" or employment. Yet we read every day in newspapers, magazines, and especially in the economic education provided as a public service by the large commercial banks and by the Federal Reserve Banks, that the wise and prudent policy is to increase the quantity of *money* by no more than some 5 percent per annum. At the current rate of price increase this is a *decrease in wage-units.*

It is such "unlearning" of a significant Keynesian lesson rather than any failure to have made a "theoretical break-through," or any failure to have found a flaw in the neo-classical logic, that would make Keynes feel not so well today. By the time he got to the end of his book Keynes seems to be giving up the idea that he has earned, or indeed that he needs, any diploma certifying a theoretical break-through or some logical innovation. His conclusion is: "Our criticism of the accepted classical theory of economics has consisted not so much in finding logical flaws in the analysis as in pointing out that its tacit assumptions are seldom or never satisfied, with the result that it cannot solve the economic problems of the actual world."[9]

Exposing the "tacit" classical assumptions to the open air leads almost automatically to their being discarded, and thus to the corollory that there is no satisfactory automatic mechanism for reaching and maintaining full employment. The practical conclusion is that the government has the responsibility, because only the government has the means, for a full employment economic policy. This lesson, though not as consistently applied, seems to be as firmly established as Adam's Law.

9. *Ibid.*, p. 378.

COMMENTS

Gordon Tullock

Abba Lerner says, "In the world of practical policy, the basic Keynesian principle – governmental responsibility for an acceptable level of employment – is very much alive and flourishing" (p. 60). Granted the fact that both the United States and England have had considerable – indeed, unprecedented since World War I – unemployment recently and that in neither case have they responded by Keynesian steps, this seems an odd statement about the world. I should say that I do not think that the failure of the government to do anything about this unemployment comes from a lack of will but from a lack of means. Unbalanced budgets and other demand-stimulating mechanisms no longer seem to work. Indeed, if we look at the results of just the last three or four years, one could argue that deflation leads to reduced unemployment and inflation leads to increasing unemployment. Obviously, I do not argue that this cause and effect relationship is correct, but I do say that our recent performance raises grave doubts as to whether the Keynesian remedies will still cure.

Further evidence along these lines, reproduced below in Figure 1, is a Phillips curve diagram in which the data are all drawn from the United States between 1965 and 1975. The data were grouped by two-year instead of one-year periods, and the best fit (ordinary least-squares) lines of regression between these two variables was computed. It will be observed that it slopes upward to the right, instead of downward to the left. If we believed this established an empirical relationship (needless to say, I do not), we would be "counter-Keynesians."

In fact, what is happening is that the Phillips curve still has the usual shape, but it is rapidly shifting toward the vertical and moving out to the right and upward. This time trend dominates the observations, and we get the rather odd empirical Phillips curve of the figure. Still, the answer to the question of what we should do under these circumstances is not very plain from the Lerner paper.

The only real reference to the present situation in which inflation does not seem to be reducing unemployment in Lerner's paper is the discussion of the wage unit standard at the very end. These remarks are somewhat nonoperational because it is impossible to

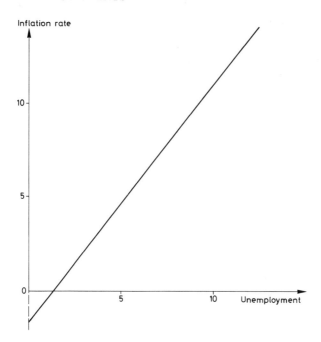

Figure 1. Phillips Curve − U. S., 1965−1975.

OLSQ equation

$$INF = -1.44 \quad + 1.485UE$$
$$(-.5003)^* \quad (2.5299)^*$$

$$R^2 = .68, F(.05; 1,3) = 6.4^*$$

*F and t-statistics, both of which are insignificant at 5% level.

tell exactly what the wage unit is at any point in time.[1] Workers can obviously increase their wage unit to any desired rate and, in particular, in an inflationary period they may choose to use a price index, at which point it becomes impossible to affect the wage unit at all by inflationary means.

Keynes once said that in the long run we are all dead. As Rothbard has said, Keynes is dead, but we are now alive. What has happened, in essence, is that the long run − as seen from the

---

1. In oral discussion, Lerner, on being challenged to say what conceivable observation might disprove the Keynesian wage unit theory, said that if inflation were 80 percent and there were still unemployment, he would concede that the cause of the unemployment was not inadequate demand.

perspective of the 1930s — is now with us. A policy of wiping out unemployment by progressively increasing doses of inflation has taught the workers about real incomes and the money illusion. Investors, similarly, have learned that there is something called the "real" interest rate, as well as the money interest rate. Under these circumstances, the Keynesian tools — and, it must also be said, the monetary tools — lose their effect. That they would do so was foreseen in the 1930s; the only problem was when would the short run end. This was indeed a hard problem *ex ante*, but *ex post* we have no great difficulties with it.

It does not seem possible that present-day unemployment can be the result of inadequate demand. Indeed, if it were, the fact that unemployment is falling in almost perfect step with the rate of inflation would be impossible to explain. As it happens, in the week before Lerner read his paper and this comment was presented, newspapers reported both the lowest rate of inflation in years and the lowest rate of unemployment in years. How does a Keynesian (or, for that matter, a monetarist) explain this?

It seems certain that the causes of unemployment must be more than one. There is no doubt that a great deal of unemployment has been caused in the past by deflations. It seems likely, however, (and our present experience is not explicable in any other terms) that there are other causes of unemployment. What we need is research to determine what these causes are and to develop remedies for them. This research will not be attempted in the space of this brief comment, but I would like to suggest one particular project, drawn from the history of Lerner's native England. The 1920s were a period of high unemployment in England. Economic historians, however, say that if you discard the high unemployment, it was basically a prosperous and progressive period. Most of the histories have tended to blame the unemployment of the 1920s on the deflationary policies followed by the government. These policies, however, were not followed throughout the period; and, in any event, one would have thought the market would have adjusted to them in a 10-year period. Some other cause of unemployment seems a likely object of historical research.

The years from 1945 to the mid-1960s were, in essence, the mirror image of the 1920s. This was a period of astonishingly low unemployment, together with a general low level of economic growth and poor economic performance. It was a classic period of stop and go, with the government alternately attempting to expand and then sharply contracting demand. One would have thought that this policy would have led to high unemployment about every two years during the contractionary phase of this very short but very sharp business cycle. It did not. Since the mid-1960s, on the other hand, the government of England has followed a very strong expansionary policy, with unprecedentedly high rates of inflation. This has been accompanied by a high rate of unemployment, although the growth rate of the economy has certainly not been particularly distinguished.

All of this is hard to explain if we assume that monetary or fiscal factors are the basic cause of unemployment. However, there is another possible explanation. Before World War I, the bulk of the unemployed in England received no or very inadequate government payments, and in essence were supported by special unemployment funds of their trade unions. As part of the World War I social settlement, these payments were transferred to the state. I hypothesize that the dole was set too high. It seems likely, although not being a historian of the period I cannot be sure, that the basic explanation of the high unemployment all through the 1920s was simply that the unemployment compensation payments were high enough so that for many Englishmen their comparative advantage was highest working for that particular branch of the government which paid the dole.

As a result of technological progress and inflation, basic wages in 1945 (denominated in pounds sterling) were very, very much higher than they had been in the 1920s. The basic payment schedule, however, had not been raised very much. In consequence, England, to all intents and purposes, had no one who could not make a good deal more in employment (even with a poor job) than on the dole. This led to low unemployment until the mid-1960s. In the mid-1960s, unemployment benefits were sharply increased. Since that date, unemployment has always been much higher than at any time between 1945 and the mid-1960s, although in general lower than in the 1920s.

I would not like to argue that we should draw a general social law from one observation, or even that my rather causal observation of the facts in England proves that variations in unemployment compensation are the principal cause of unemployment there (except in the decade of the 1930s), but it does seem to me a

worthwhile subject for investigation. I can think of various other
explanations for unemployment, and I would suggest to the readers
that they (or their graduate students) might find the entire problem
an important one for further research. In any event, it seems to me
that the Keynesian era is now one with Ninevah and Tyre.

Melville J. Ulmer

That Lord Keynes would not be feeling well today, as Professor
Lerner suggests, is a proposition that I think most informed
observers would accept. As one called in for consultation, however,
I'd be inclined to question Dr. Lerner's diagnosis. The seat of the
Keynesian ailment, as our speaker sees it, is simply the anguish that
an earnest teacher feels in the presence of a class, or a nation, of
backward students. Apparently, in the darkness of their ignorance,
our authorities do not let the quantity of money rise faster than
wage rates – or at least they do not do so persistently and diligently
enough. It is this failure, Professor Lerner contends, that brings
upon us our periodical recessions; and it is this misunderstanding of
this theory that induces Lord Keynes' psychosomatic illness.

I would contend that the Keynesian illness is not psychosomatic
at all, but that it springs from a congenital maladjustment in the
body of his theory. If so, the disease would not call for a
psychiatrist, but a surgeon.

In the limited time I have, I'm not going to deal with a possible
cure, but rather present my version of the diagnosis, and even that,
in abbreviated form. I start with one fact that I believe is
indisputable. Keynesian policies have been in practice, more or less,
since the end of World War II in the United States. I grant that it
has often been fumbling, and in the 1950s it was executed with a
becoming anonymity, because of the popular association, in those
warped days, between the name of Keynes and those of Stalin,
Hitler, Attila and other famous murderers. The important fact, as
derived from that experience, is that every time the economy was
encouraged to expand, wages and prices rose. Now these inflations
were not all suggestive of the gentle rise in prices, prompted by
increasing marginal costs, temporary bottlenecks, and perhaps some
union activity, that Keynes thought would accompany an approach
to the full employment level that his policies would guarantee. The
inflations in our experience were cyclical, accelerating, and cumula-

tive. Furthermore, they left a distinctly unKeynesian aftertaste. Even when business activity declined, wages and prices continued to advance, albeit at a slower pace. In addition, there has been a clear tendency for the successive inflations to grow progressively worse. That is, if we grant the existence of a Phillips curve, at least as an instantaneous relationship, the curve has moved rapidly to the north east. And of course it has been these accelerating inflations that in every case has led government to shut off the economic expansions, in most instances before full employment was very closely approached. The question I now pose is, why wasn't this difficulty foreseen in the Keynesian theory?

I believe the answer is that in this portion of his thinking – that is, in discussing the promotion of economic expansions – Keynes made two implicit assumptions that obscured his vision. He reasoned *as though* business and labor markets were perfectly competitive. He also reasoned as though labor were homogeneous. Yet the facts to the contrary are what lie at the bottom of the contemporary inflation-unemployment dilemma.

Now I want to skip much of what I hope may be obvious, and offer some possible explanations for what I believe is the most puzzling aspect of the problem: that is, the failure of wages and prices to decline in recessions, and – in fact, except for 1949 – their persistent and perverse tendency to rise even during the stiffest economic contractions. My hypothesis is that this behavior is not misguided, as some suggest, but is entirely rational from the standpoint of the decision-making units involved. In his recent AEA presidential address, Robert A. Gordon remarks that "we economists pay too little attention to the *changing* institutional environment that conditions economic behavior." He italicized the word changing. The critical change in the period now under review was the Keynesian stabilization technique itself. Its unofficial, and later official adoption by government meant, at least so far as people then could see, that declines in business activity would never again be allowed to progress very far or last very long. That conviction was bound to influence the behavior of business and labor.

In a word, oligopolistic industry and organized labor have both learned, as Wall Street puts it, to look across the valley, a tendency that for them automatically increases the risk of deflationary tactics and reduces the risk of those promoting inflation. For example, a price or wage reduction in recession might well entail a larger increase than would otherwise be necessary in the next upswing. Such dramatic shifts in prices could be psychologically disturbing to buyers just when new profit opportunities appear. For labor, a subsequent attempt to secure what would appear to be too large a wage increase, in one lump during the expansion, could alienate public and governmental support. Fortifying these reasons for resisting a drop in either prices or wages, during recession, are the many rigid elements in the structure of costs, the alternative income sources now open to workers, such as generous unemployment insurance, and above all, the fact that oligopolistic industries fear the appearance of a price war even more than they would a battalion of Ralph Naders.

But beyond these general considerations there is one particular characteristic of contemporary recessions that not only discourages declines, but positively encourages increases in prices and wages. In most textbooks dealing with price formation, recessions are depicted simply by a decline in demand, which could be expected to depress the price for a profit-maximizing firm, especially if it is complemented by a decline in costs, and especially if we neglect the dynamic considerations just mentioned. But in many important industries, demand not only declines but changes its shape, so as to become over a substantial range highly inelastic. Buyers who remain buyers in recession are frequently just of two limited types. First there are those whose needs are not postponable — as were people with superannuated cars in 1974 and 1975, or a household with an ancient or broken refrigerator, or a manufacturer with a machine in that condition. Second are the fortunate and usually affluent households or business concerns whose financial resources remain undiminished in recession, of which in modern times there are a great many. In neither group are purchases likely to be materially discouraged by a modest price increase. Facing inelastic demands, within limits, profits rise if prices do — and of course they do! And note that if demand is inelastic for output, the derived demand for input is likely to be inelastic too, in the short run. That is an open invitation for higher wages.

Against this background, the economic as well as psychological basis is laid for the increasing intensity of inflations during upswings. But time permits reference to just one significant aspect of that phenomenon that has received too little attention. I return here to the previously mentioned peril of treating labor as though it were homogeneous. There is in fact a critical split in the labor force, and I refer not to females versus males, and certainly not blacks versus whites, since 75 or 80 percent of the unemployed are normally white. The split in question has to do with the level of skills. A very large part of the labor force remains virtually unaffected by recessions. You can tell this by examining BLS data on unemployment rates by occupation. The jobless rates remain at 1, 2, or 2½ percent in recessions for nearly all skilled workers, professionals, administrators, technicians, and of course government employees. You can tell this also by simply noting stories in the *Wall Street Journal*, reporting severe shortages of what is always considered a surprising variety of skills even during our worst recessions. Meanwhile, of course, among the unskilled and semi-skilled, unemployment rates during downturns are anywhere between 2 and 4 times the national average. Now, when we use the famed Keynesian techniques for expanding demand and employment, we create what can only be called *over*full employment in markets for the more skilled workers, the technicians, professionals, and other favored personnel − an inflationary situation in which jobs are chasing men − and women. At the time time, the unskilled and semi-skilled are helped only modestly. This is, I think, a seriously neglected, contributing factor in the periodic but frustrating efforts our nation has made to achieve or approach full employment. It means that if functional finance is to work, something new, different, and important must be added. Macroeconomic policies alone won't do. That is also another reason why Keynes, were he alive, would not be feeling so well today.

5. THE POLITICAL BIASES OF KEYNESIAN ECONOMICS

James M. Buchanan and Richard E. Wagner*

5.1. Introduction

Once upon a time it was generally believed that, so long as prevailing institutions constrained monetary excesses, a free-enterprise economy was self-adjusting within broad cyclical limits. Movements away from a fully employed economy would set in motion corrective forces that operated to restore prosperity. One source of disturbance was thought to be the profligacy of government, and it was considered important that governmental proclivities in this respect be constrained. A balanced budget was one of the practical rules that reflected such constraints. The advent of what has been called "Keynesian Economics" changed all this. The Keynesian vision was one in which monetary management could not produce a self-correcting economy; more extensive discretionary management which included fiscal policy was required to ensure peak performance. Such discretionary management necessarily required eradication of the principled adherence to balanced budget norms of fiscal conduct. The scope of the Keynesian conversion was wide indeed. It extended all the way from purely academic controversy about Say's Law to real-world practices about whether public expenditures should be limited to the tax revenues raised to finance those expenditures. In this paper we suggest that the explicit Keynesian destruction of the rigid balanced budget rule produced a political bias in the conduct of economic policy in a democratic society, and, moreover, that this bias operates to some extent to make the Keynesian prophecies self-fulfilling.[1]

The acceptance of Keynesian ideas by the politicians and the general voting public is often dated from the onset of the 1960s. The fiscal record of the 16 years after 1961 tells its own story. Between 1961 and 1976, there was only one year of budget surplus for the federal government. The 15 years of deficit totalled some $240 billion. Moreover, the annual deficits increased in magnitude over this period. For 1961-68, the cumulative deficit was $60 billion; for 1970-74, it was $67 billion, and for the two-year period, 1975-76, more than $110 billion.

We observe a dramatic increase in the relative size of government over this period, accompanied by inflation unmatched in other than war periods. Total governmental expenditures increased from somewhat less than one-third of National Income (from 32.8 percent) in 1960, to a little more than two-fifths (40.4 percent) of National Income in 1974. The consumer price index rose by 92.3 percent over this same period, and accelerated more or less in step with the size of the federal deficits.

At a preliminary level of discussion, the effects of Keynesian economic policy on the democratic politics of budgetary choice seem simple and straight forward, whether treated in terms of plausible behavioral hypotheses or of observable political reality. Elected politicians enjoy spending public monies on projects that return benefits to their constituents. They do not enjoy imposing taxes on these same constituents. The pre-Keynesian norm of budget balance served to constrain spending proclivities so as to keep budgets roughly within the revenue limits generated by taxes.[2] The Keynesian destruction of this norm, without an adequate replacement, effectively removed the constraint. Predictably, politicians responded by increasing spending more than tax revenues, by generating budget deficits as a normal course of events.

1. While this paper was written first, this theme about what might be called the political economy of Keynesian economics is elaborated and refined in our previously published book: *Democracy in Deficit: The Political Legacy of Lord Keynes* (New York: Academic Press, 1977).

2. During the 14-year period, 1947-60, there were seven years of deficit and seven years of surplus. And the total budget was roughly balanced over this period, with the deficits summing to $31.2 billion and the surpluses amounting to $30.2 billion. This summary result becomes even more significant when it is recalled that the Korean War is included in the period covered.

They did not live up to the apparent Keynesian precepts; they did not match the deficits of recession with the surpluses of boom. The simple logic of Keynesian fiscal policy has demonstrably failed in its institutional application to democratic politics.[3] The accumulating record is available for all to see.

At a more fundamental level of discussion, however, many issues arise. Why do politicians behave in the way indicated? Public choice theory tells us that they do so largely in the expectation that voters will support them. But this merely shifts attention to the behavior of the voters. Why do voters support politicians who behave "irresponsibly" in the fiscal sense? What is there about the acceptance of Keynesian economics that generates the fiscal experience witnessed in the years after 1961? There is a paradox of sorts here. A regime of continuous and mounting deficits, with subsequent inflation, along with a bloated public sector, can scarcely be adjudged beneficial to anyone other than the employees of the federal bureaucracy. Yet why does the working of ordinary democratic process seemingly produce such a regime, and with little hope of basic reform? Where is the institutional breakdown?

In order to examine these questions, we must recognize that neither the economic nor the political setting is that which was presumed to exist by Keynes himself. The underlying economic realities are not those of the 1930s or those that are implicitly assumed as parameters for the application of Keynesian policy norms. Furthermore, the political process within which these norms are to be applied bears little or no resemblance to that which was implicit in Keynes' basic analysis.

We shall first examine the economic *and* the political environment that is presumed for the idealized Keynesian theory of economic policy. Since the economic setting here has been exhaustively discussed, our own treatment can be brief and without detail. Although the discussion can similarly be brief, we find it necessary to emphasize the Keynesian political environment, both because this aspect of Keynesian thought has been almost totally neglected by economists and because of its importance for our central purpose.

We shall then modify the political setting by introducing

3. Our treatment of the policy implications of "Keynesian economics," is not meant to disparage the strict "economics of Keynes." On this, see Axel Leijonhufvud, *On Keynesian Economics and the Economics of Keynes* (London: Oxford University Press, 1968).

democratic political institutions; we shall examine the applicability of Keynesian policy norms within this setting. In this analysis (which might be called a public choice approach to Keynesian economics) we distinguish between an economy that is essentially Keynesian and an economy that is distinctly non-Keynesian.

We shall conclude the paper with a brief discussion of the fiscal constitution. In an Appendix, we examine critically the Ricardian analytical perspective which, unlike our own, is distinctly non-Keynesian in that it asserts the irrelevance of institutional forms on individual behavior. In contrast, we acknowledge the impact of institutions on behavior, and, indeed, it is this very impact that generates the political biases of Keynesian economics.

5.2. The Idealized Environment for Keynesian Economic Policy

Lord Keynes claimed that his was a "general theory," and it is surely correct to say that this claim of generality was influential in generating the "Keynesian revolution," especially in the thinking of professional economists. And in the textbooks on Keynesian macroeconomics that emerged after World War II, the generality of the Keynesian message for economic management was stressed. Keynesian management, it was alleged, could prevent or constrain both depression and inflation, and could be employed so as to promote a more stable economy than would be possible under any regime of monetary management.

The Economy in Depression

Soon after 1936, however, critical evaluation of Keynes' basic contribution concentrated on the setting-constrained applicability of the explanatory potential of the theory. The underlying model of the national economy is one of deep depression, and specifically an economy in which policy-induced shifts in aggregate demand can increase real output and employment *without* any effects on price levels. In the elementary diagrams of the early post-Keynesian textbooks, the aggregate supply function was horizontal out to some level of income defined to be that which would generate "full employment." In this setting, the economy is also characterized by an excess of monetary liquidity. Interest rates are at their minimal levels; economic policy which aims at increasing liquidity through increases in the supply of money alone is ineffective.

The policy implication is clear and simple. Effective demand may be increased only by increased spending, and this can be accomplished only if government increases its rate of outlays relative to its rate of revenue withdrawal from the economy. Deficit creation by government offers the only available means of increasing output and employment. The budget deficit may be financed either by money creation or by the issue of public debt instruments. Ideally, money creation is preferable, because of the absence of interest payments. But due to the excessive liquidity in the economy, the sale of bonds will not crowd out any potential private outlays, so that, aside from the minimal interest charges, the issue of debt becomes equivalent to money creation. The means of financing the deficit is unimportant; the critical element is the creation of the deficit and the enhanced rate of total spending in the economy that it facilitates.

The Symmetry of Policy Under Keynesian Political Presuppositions

As noted, Keynes claimed to present a "general theory," and particularly one that contained policy norms applicable to any underlying position of the economy. In this respect, the policy precepts of Keynesian economics were alleged to be wholly symmetrical. Under the existence of depressed conditions, budget deficits were required to restore full employment and prosperity. But when inflation rather than depression seemed to be the danger, budget surpluses were equally advised as the appropriate policy instruments. The time-honored norm of budget balance was, of course, jettisoned, but there was, in the pure logic of Keynesian policy, no one-way departure. The use of the government's budget was a two-edged weapon.

Fiscal policy was equally effective in constraining inflation or depression. Monetary policy, by contrast, was alleged to be asymmetrical. In a depression, monetary policy was deemed to be largely if not wholly ineffective. In an inflationary environment, however, monetary policy could, if desired, be utilized either as a complement to or as a substitute for the restrictive fiscal policy that the creation of budget surpluses represents.

Although particular policy instruments were viewed as asymmetrical, the application of public policy was considered to be fully symmetrical. During depression, the stream of expenditures should be expanded; during inflation, the stream of expenditures should be contracted. In both cases, rational public policy would operate to promote a more prosperous and stable economy.

The Presuppositions of Harvey Road

The idealized economic setting for the symmetrical application of Keynesian theory and policy, sketched out above, is familiar. Much less so is the political choice setting within which the policy is to be formulated and implemented. Keynes was writing directly for his professional colleagues, the economists. But he was aiming, indirectly, for modification in the policies of national governments. It is essential that we look quite closely at his assumptions about the men who choose for the nation and about the processes through which their decisions are made.

There is relatively little mystery about Keynes' own views. He was an elitist, and he was operating under what his biographer called the "presuppositions of Harvey Road," the presuppositions that governmental policy, and economic policy in particular, was made and should be made by a relatively small group of wise and enlightened men, whether in Whitehall or in Washington.[4] Keynes did not think about the application of his policy norms in what we would, in America, call a democratic setting. The small group of enlightened men who made economic policy would tend to act in accordance with the "public interest," even when this might run afoul of constituency pressures.

In the combined economic and political environment suggested, there could be little or no question raised about the application of the Keynesian policy instruments. In order to secure a stable, prosperous economy, expenditures would be expanded and contracted symmetrically. Budget deficits would be created during periods of sluggish economic activity, and surpluses would be created as the pace of economic activity accelerated. There would

---

4. "We have seen that he [Keynes] was strongly imbued with what I have called the presuppositions of Harvey Road. One of these presuppositions may perhaps be summarized in the idea that the government of Britain was and would continue to be in the hands of an intellectual aristocracy using the method of persuasion." R. F. Harrod, *The Life of John Maynard Keynes* (London: Macmillan, 1951), pp. 192–193.

be no political pressures operating to render the surpluses fictive and the deficits disproportionately large or ill-timed. The ruling elite would be guided by the presuppositions of Harvey Road; they would not act as competitors in a democratic political environment. Moreover, no bias need be introduced as between public and private sectors because the appropriate dividing line would continue to be determined by the same group of wise men guided by their own vision of the broader public interest of the community as a whole.

5.3 Generalized Political Implications of Keynesian Economics

The discussion in the preceding section has been necessary both for analytical completeness and as background for our primary purpose. This purpose is to examine the impact of the Keynesian precepts for economic policy in a political decision structure that is different in kind from that which was envisaged by Keynes himself, and in an economic environment that is demonstrably non-Keynesian. Political decisions in the United States are made by elected politicians, who respond to the desires and demands of voters. There is no center of power where an enlightened few can effectively isolate themselves from continuing constituency pressures. Furthermore, since World War II the national economy has never been appropriately described as being in depression of the sort idealized in the elementary Keynesian models. Throughout the three decades of postwar experience, increases in aggregate demand have always been accompanied by increases in price levels, by inflation. Upward shifts in aggregate demand have also been normally accompanied by increases in real output and employment, although this basic relationship has been increasingly called into question since the mid-1960s.

Keynesian policy is centered on the use of the government's budget as the primary instrument for insuring the maintenance of high employment and output. The implementation of Keynesian policy, therefore, required both the destruction of former principles of balanced public budgets and the replacement of those principles by principles that permitted the imbalance that was necessary for Keynesian budgetary manipulation. But politicians, and the public generally, were not urged, by Keynes or the Keynesians, to introduce deficit spending without a supporting logical argument.

There was more to the "Keynesian revolution" than mere destruction of the balanced budget principle as a permanent feature of the fiscal constitution. This destruction itself was a reasoned result of a modified paradigm of the working of an economy. And, in the larger sense, this was really what "Keynesian" is all about. The allocative bias toward a larger public sector, the monetary bias toward inflation — these biases are aspects of, and to an extent are contained within, a more comprehensive political bias of Keynesian economics, an "interventionist bias," which stems directly from the shift in paradigm.

Specifically Keynesian features emerge when the paradigm is shifted away from that which may be summarized under the expression "Say's Equality."[5] The idea that the spontaneous coordination of economic activities through a system of markets would normally produce overall stability was replaced by a vision of an economy that is inherently unstable. The new Keynesian paradigm, or rather the old Malthusian one, is that of an economy continually hounded by gluts and threatened by secular stagnation.[6] An important element in the Keynesian paradigm is the absence of an equilibrating mechanism which insures that departures from trend levels of real output growth are self-correcting. When exogenous shocks force the economy off its expansion path, no corrective devices are predicted to come into play. Hence government intervention follows, almost as a moral imperative. And there is no argument for allowing for a time period between some initially observed departures and the onset of policy action. With no conception of self-correction inherent in the accepted paradigm of the economy, "fine tuning" becomes the policy ideal.[7]

---

5. See Karl Brunner, "Knowledge, Values, and the Choice of Economic Organization," *Kyklos* 23 (Nov. 3, 1970): 558–580, for an examination of the impact of paradigms (Brunner uses the term, "orientations") which provide the framework for interpreting experiences, upon particular elements of public policy. See W. H. Hutt, *A Rehabilitation of Say's Law* (Athens, Ohio: Ohio University Press, 1974), for an interpretative survey of Say's Equality.

6. For a specific discussion of these two economic cosmologies, see Axel Leijonhufvud, "Effective Demand Failures," *Swedish Journal of Economics* 75 (March 1973): pp. 31–33.

7. A direct corollary to the view that aggregative shifts are not self-correcting is the notion, even if this is implicit, that such shifts cannot themselves be the results of distorting elements in market structure. Applied to employment, this suggests a tendency to attribute all shifts downward in observed rates of employment to fluctuations in aggregate demand. In such a policy setting, government intervention to correct for increased unemployment that is, in fact, caused by labor market dislocation and structural rigidities, acts to cement the latter into quasi-permanence and to make ultimate correction more difficult.

The notion of an unstable economy whose performance could be improved through the manipulation of public budgets produced a general principle that budgets *need not* be in balance. There would be years of deficit and there would be years of surplus, with these deficits and surpluses being necessary for, as well as indicating the enactment of, macroeconomic management. As we noted in our discussion of the Keynesian political framework, however, the Keynesian budgetary policies would be applied symmetrically. In such a political setting of rule by the Apostles of Harvey Road, it might even be said that Keynesian economics did not destroy the principle of a balanced budget, but only lengthened the time period over which it applied. The Keynesian paradigm, in other words, did not seem to change the fiscal constitution within which economic policy is conducted.

But what happens when we make non-Keynesian assumptions about politics? What if we commence from the assumption that elected politicians respond to constitutency desires? When this shift is made in the political setting for analysis, the possibilities that policy precepts may contain political biases cannot be ignored. On this score, it should be noted, Keynes' own biographer seemed prescient, for in continuing his discussion of the presuppositions of Harvey Road he mused:

> If, owing to the needs of planning, the functions of government became very far-reaching and multifarious, would it be possible for the intellectual aristocracy to remain in essential control? Keynes tended till the end to think of the really important decisions being reached by a small group of intelligent people, like the group that fashioned the Bretton Woods plan. But would not a democratic government having a wide multiplicity of duties tend to get out of control and act in a way of which the intelligent would not approve? This is another dilemma – how to reconcile the functioning of a planning and interfering democracy with the requirement that in the last resort the best considered judgment should prevail. It may be that the presuppositions of Harvey Road were so much of a second nature to Keynes that he did not give this dilemma the full consideration which it deserves.[8]

5.4. Unbalanced Budgets and Democratic Politics

In a democracy, political competition is not unlike market competition. Politicians compete among themselves for the support

8. Harrod, *op. cit.*, p. 193.

of the electorate, and they do so by offering policies and programs which they feel will get them elected or reelected. A politician in a democratic society can be viewed as proposing and attempting to enact a combination of expenditure programs and financing schemes that secures him the support of a majority of the electorate.

The variety of avenues for modeling the emergence of budgetary policy in a democratic political system are considerable. A government can provide a single service, or it can provide a combination of services. It can finance its budget by a variety of tax forms, either singly or in combination, and, additionally, it can subject any particular tax to a variety of rate schedules and exemption rules. Furthermore, preferences for public services can differ as among individual citizens, particular features of the political system can vary, and budget imbalance can be permitted.

Changes in any of these particular features will normally change the budgetary outcomes that emerge. Changes in tax institutions, for instance, will normally change the tax shares and tax prices assigned to different persons. This, in turn, will alter individual responses to particular budgetary patterns. The number of services provided may also matter. With a single service, it is fruitful to conceptualize budgetary outcomes in a plurality electoral system as conforming to the preferences of the median voter. With multiple services, however, the conceptualization is not necessarily so simple, for a trading of votes may take place among persons over issues.

To illustrate, consider the choice of budget size in a democracy operating under a balanced budget constraint. Let a single service be provided, start with a budget of zero, and take account of the gains and losses in terms of constituent support from expansions in the size of the budget. Under the assumption that the public service enters positively into the utility functions of citizens, the expenditure by itself will secure support for the politician. The taxes, however, will reduce the disposable income of citizens, thereby affecting them negatively and reducing support for the politician. In a plurality electoral system, for given preferences and fixed tax institutions, the budget will be expanded so long as a majority would prefer the public service to the private goods they have to sacrifice via taxation.[9]

A full modeling of political competition in a democratic society can become quite complex. Nonetheless, the central notions we have just described are sufficient for our purposes in this paper.[10] What this line of analysis suggests is that the consideration by politicians of the gains and losses in terms of constituent support of alternative taxing and spending programs shapes the budgetary outcomes that emerge within a democratic system of political competition. The size and composition of public budgets in such a system of competitive democracy, in other words, can be viewed as a product of the preferences of a politician's constituents and the constitutional-institutional rules that constrain the political system.

With a balanced budget rule, any proposal for expenditure must be coupled with a proposal for taxation. What would happen if the requirement of budget balance were eliminated? What would be the nature of the pressures of political competition in such a revised, Keynesian constitutional setting? We shall first consider a budget surplus, and then a budget deficit. For each of these cases, we shall also distinguish whether the economic environment is Keynesian or non-Keynesian.

Budget Surpluses and Democratic Politics

The creation of a budget surplus requires an increase in tax collections without a corresponding increase in public spending, or a decrease in the latter without a corresponding decrease in the former. What political pressures result from such budgetary policies? We must distinguish between the direct or immediate and the indirect or secondary pressures. Directly, budget surpluses create no gainers, only losers, regardless of whether the economy is Keynesian or non-Keynesian. In an inflationary setting, of course, the Keynesian and the non-Keynesian policy precepts are identical. In this setting, a policy of budget surplus requires individuals to pay more taxes than before, but without any compensating increase in public output. (Or, to suffer cuts in public outlays, with no reductions in tax burden.)

9. Anthony Downs, *An Economic Theory of Democracy* (New York: Harper & Row, 1957), pp. 51–74, suggested that the size of the budget in a democracy can be viewed as the outcome of a process in which politicians continue to expand the budget so long as the marginal vote gain from public expenditure exceeds the marginal vote loss from the taxation required to finance the expenditure.
10. For a recent, thorough survey of the literature on the properties of political competition, see William H. Riker and Peter C. Ordeshook, *An Introduction to Positive Political Theory* (Englewood Cliffs, N. J.: Prentice-Hall, 1973).

It could be argued that a sophisticated citizenry should be able to see beyond the direct considerations to the indirect ones. They should understand that a budget surplus was required to prevent inflation, and that this was beneficial. The dissipation of a surplus through public spending or tax cuts, therefore, would not be costless, for it would destroy those benefits that would result from the control of inflation.

Informationally, the requirements for citizens to understand and evaluate the indirect benefits they receive from budget surpluses are stringent. In order for the indirect benefits from budget surpluses to offset fully the absence of direct benefits, it would be necessary for citizens to know fully what is at stake in choosing between politicians who propose to spend the revenues that might otherwise generate a potential budget surplus and politicians who propose to generate the surplus by holding down public outlays. Citizens would have to understand how the surplus would operate in restraining inflationary forces in the aggregate, and they would also have to be able to relate this restraint to a personal level of benefit. That is, it would be necessary for citizens to interpret the aggregate economy in precisely the manner that it is interpreted by the economists (*if only they provided a single interpretation*), as well as to develop a relation between this aggregative pattern and their own personal well-being. The very intensity of controversy among economists over precisely such matters, however, attests to the extreme unreasonableness of such requirements. Therefore, it is likely that the benefits of a budgetary surplus in restraining inflation will to some extent be underestimated by the citizenry.[11]

Even if all citizens were able to reach the same, "correct" interpretation, matters of incentive arise that reinforce the likelihood that a surplus would not be created, or, if created, would be smaller than it would be in a world of full knowledge. Knowledge does not come freely, however, but must be sought after. At the very least, it would be necessary to pursue some line of textbook-type argumentation. This is not a costless activity for the citizen, so the amount of knowledge attained will depend upon the incentives to acquire such knowledge. The costs are apparent, but what are the gains? Most likely, "nothing," and at best, "very little." In politics,

11. This line of argument is explained in Buchanan and Wagner, *Democracy in Deficit*, pp. 125–144.

unlike in the market place, no one person is able to change his personal actions, and through this his personal economic position, in response to changes in knowledge. Rather, personal positions can change only as a majority of citizens decide to act differently, only as the collective-decision process generates different policies. What this consideration suggests is that the gain to any one person of securing knowledge in these matters is practically zero.[12]

Budget surpluses would seem to have weaker survival prospects in a political democracy than in a social order controlled by "wise men." This difference in political viability can also be seen by approaching the matter in the opposite direction. Consider the comparative properties of the creation of a budget surplus and a proposal to utilize the surplus-creating revenue, through tax reduction, through expenditure increases, or through some combination of these. The second of these alternatives would clearly offer direct, immediate, and apparent gains, not losses. Politically, one such proposal would dominate a program of budget surplus creation. The surplus would benefit no one directly, and, would impose direct costs on some if not all of the population; on the other hand, the use of the revenues that might generate the surplus would directly benefit some if not all of the citizens. To the extent that the indirect costs and gains are understood only imperfectly, as they clearly are, actions will tend to be based on the direct costs and gains. Budget surpluses may emerge in a democratic political system, but considerations of information and incentive both operate to suggest that the institutional biases against such surpluses are strong indeed.

---

12. And even to the extent that citizens do possess such knowledge, democratic budgetary processes may be incapable of acting upon it. The extent to which such action will be forthcoming depends on the nature of budgetary institutions. To the extent that budgetary institutions permit fragmented appropriations, for instance, a prisoner's dilemma will tend to operate to dissipate revenues that might produce a budget surplus, even though citizens understand fully the benefits of surplus creation. Suppose, for instance, that a potential $10 billion budget surplus is prevented from arising through 10 separate spending proposals of $1 billion each, as opposed to a single expenditure proposal of $10 billion. In the first case, although each participant may recognize that he would be better off if none of the spending proposals carry, institutions that allow separate, fragmented budgetary consideration may operate to create a result that is mutually undesirable, akin to the familiar prisoner's dilemma. For an analysis of this, see James M. Buchanan and Gordon Tullock, *The Calculus of Consent* (Ann Arbor: University of Michigan Press, 1962), especially Chapter 10.

Budget Deficits and Democratic Politics.

In a democratic society, there are no obstacles to budget deficits in a Keynesian economic setting. Budget deficits make it possible to spend without taxing. Whether the deficit is created through reduced taxes or increased expenditures, and the particular forms of each, will, of course, determine the distribution of gains among citizens. The central point of importance, however, is that, directly, there are only gainers from such deficits, not losers. In the true Keynesian setting, of course, this is as it should be. A political democracy will pose no obstacles to deficit spending in a Keynesian economy.

It is possible, however, for political bias to emerge in the decisions over the appropriate public sector-private sector mix. If the introduction of deficit financing creates signals for taxpayers that public services have become relatively cheaper than before, voters will demand a shift in the composition of real output toward publicly provided services. The "true" opportunity costs of public goods relative to private goods will not, of course, be modified by the use of the budget for purposes of stabilization. To the extent that voters, and their elected legislators, can recognize these "true" cost ratios, no public spending bias need be introduced. It does not, however, seem at all plausible to suggest that voters can dispel the illusion of a relative price change as between public and private goods.[13]

Consider the following highly simplified example. In the full employment equilibrium assumed to have been in existence before an unanticipated shortfall in aggregate demand, the government provided *one* unit of a public good, and financed this with a tax of *$1*. The restoration of full employment requires a monetary-fiscal response of *10 cents*. Suppose now that the response takes the form of reducing tax rates. Taxes fall so that only *90 cents* is collected, while *$1* continues to be spent. The tax price per unit of public output is only 90 percent of its former levels. At any tax-price elasticity greater than zero, equilibrium in the "market" for the public good can be restored only by some increase in quantity beyond *one unit*, with the precise magnitude of the increase being

---

13. We should note that the preceding discussion of budget surplus would be subject to the reverse relative price change from that discussed here.

dependent on the value of the elasticity coefficient. So long as individuals concentrate attention on the value of public goods, defined in the numeraire, there will be a clear bias toward expanding the size of the public sector in real terms, despite the presumed absence of any underlying shift in tastes.[14]

The results here require that individuals confront tax-prices that remain invariant over quantities of public goods financed. That is to say, marginal tax-price must equal average tax-price. Institutionally, this requirement is met with most of the familiar tax instruments: proportional and progressive income taxation, sales taxation, property taxation. Tax reductions are normally discussed, and implemented, through reductions in rates of tax applied to the defined base. So long as a deficit-facilitated tax cut takes this form, the terms-of-trade between public goods and private goods will seem to shift in favor of the former. The institutionally-generated illusion, and the public-goods bias that results from it, can be dispelled if marginal tax-prices are somehow held constant while tax collections are reduced inframarginally. If a deficit-facilitated tax cut could take this latter form, there would be no substitution effect brought into play: individuals would continue to confront the same public goods-private goods trade-off, *at the margin*, before and after the fiscal-policy shift.[15]

Deficit finance in a Keynesian economic setting, while possibly altering the public-private mix in the economy because of the generation of false signals, is unlikely to encounter political obstructions. This is quite unlike a policy of surplus finance in the converse inflationary setting. On the contrary, the problem with deficit finance is that once the constitutional requirement of budget

14. The model summarized here is essentially equivalent to the one analyzed more fully in James M. Buchanan, "Fiscal Policy and Fiscal Preference," *Public Choice*, II (1967), pp.1–10; Reprinted in *Theory of Public Choice*, edited by James M. Buchanan and Robert D. Tollison (Ann Arbor: University of Michigan Press, 1972), pp. 76–84.
15. It is difficult to construct permanent institutional arrangements that will meet the marginal tax-price criterion suggested here. Our colleague, T. N. Tideman, has reminded us, however, that, for temporary tax cuts, a pure rebate scheme does accomplish the purpose. Such action does not modify tax rates *ex ante*, and, hence, marginal tax-prices. A pure rebate scheme that is not anticipated offers an allocatively-neutral scheme of injecting new currency into an economy during a temporary lapse into a pure Keynesian setting. If, however, the spending shortfall is expected to be permanent, and to require continuing injections, rebates will come to violate allocational neutrality for the familiar reasons. As soon as persons come to anticipate the *ex post* rebates in making their budgetary decisions *ex ante*, they will act as if marginal tax-prices are reduced. To forestall the public sector spending bias in this permanent setting, some other institutional means of maintaining constancy in marginal tax-prices would have to be invented.

balance is removed, there are pressures for budget deficits, even in wholly inappropriate non-Keynesian economic settings. If we assume that the money supply is at all elastic in response, budget deficits must be inflationary in a non-Keynesian setting.[16] As with budget surpluses, the indirect effects of inflation will create losers. The information and incentive effects, however, will operate to soften the strength of these indirect effects. The direct effects, by contrast, will create only gainers, for public spending can be increased without taxation, or taxation can be reduced without reductions in public spending, or some combination of the two.

There are no obstacles to budget deficits, then, in a Keynesian economic setting. But when budget deficits are permitted in a democratic society, pressures for deficits in a non-Keynesian setting are created, pressures that would not exist in a Keynesian political setting. Therefore, the removal of a balanced budget principle or constitutional rule in a political democracy ultimately will generate an asymmetry in the conduct of budgetary policy. The deficits will be created, but to a greater extent than justified by the Keynesian principles; while surpluses may sometimes result, they will result less frequently than required by the Keynesian prescriptions.[17]

When the inappropriateness of the Keynesian political setting is acknowledged, it becomes apparent that the Keynesian paradigm does indeed alter the underlying fiscal constitution. The result has been a tendency toward budget deficits and, consequently, once the workings of democratic political institutions are taken into account, inflation. The Keynesian economic paradigm creates an inflationary

16. See Buchanan and Wagner, *Democracy in Deficit* pp. 107–124, for an examination from a public choice perspective of the relation between deficit financing and monetary changes.
17. Grade inflation in colleges and universities offers a useful analogy. An analogue to a balanced budget rule might require a professor to apportion a fixed number of points among his students. A university that desired a 2.5 grade point average, for instance, would allocate 125 points to a professor who had 50 students. In this setting, a professor, in order to give more points to one student, would have to take away points from another student. With a variable number of points, however, a professor could run a surplus by giving out fewer than 125 points, or he could run a deficit by giving out more than 125 points. Before student evaluations, tight educational budgets, and related matters, the professor was in the position of the elite of Harvey Road. He was immune from political pressures in making choices that resulted in particular grade distributions. Political pressures have intensified in recent years. Budget surpluses (low grade point averages) have little survival power, and budget deficits (high grade point averages) are a natural outcome, so long as external constraints are not imposed, for a higher grade to any particular student is essentially costless to the professor, and generally yields benefits to him. Grade inflation and currency inflation, then, seem to have much in common.

bias in a democratic setting: governments respond more vigorously in correcting for unemployment than in correcting for inflation. The one-sided application of Keynesian policy remedies, which emerges from a democratic political setting, may itself create instability in the process. Inflation, it has increasingly been realized, does not generate employment. In fact, inflation attracts resources into employments where they cannot be maintained without further inflation.[18] The inflationary biases of the Keynesian paradigm, therefore, may well be able to convert a non-Keynesian economic environment into a Keynesian one. In this fashion, Keynesian prescriptions applied in a non-Keynesian setting can create a self-fulfilling prophecy. Yet Lord Keynes himself was strongly aware and quite fearful of the long term destructive consequences of inflation. Keynes, as we have noted, did not envisage a democratic political setting. But Keynesianism changed the fiscal constitution, and did so in a pro-inflationary manner.

5.5. The Fiscal Constitution

The arguments of the two preceding sections were designed to demonstrate that the institutions through which fiscal choices are made can, in themselves, exert important influences on these choices, and, further, that the direction of effect can be predicted from a careful analysis of such institutions. If these arguments are accepted, the existence of political biases derivative from the application of Keynesian economic policy rules in democracy cannot readily be denied. This is because it could scarcely be claimed that the abandonment of budget-balance represented no change in the basic institutions of fiscal choice. Indeed, the change in institutions was hailed as the instrumental step in the Keynesian policy package.

If our analysis is accepted, therefore, we should not be surprised at the post-1960 fiscal record. Once the last vestiges of the old-time

18. See Friedrich A. Hayek, *Prices and Production*, 2nd ed. (London: Routledge and Kegan Paul, 1935), for an early though neglected explanation of this theme. It should perhaps be noted that Hayek developed his analysis in terms of an excessive attraction of resources into the production of capital goods. This resulted from monetary expansion which drove the market rate of interest below the real rate. In these days of massive public spending, however, the story is more complex, for the objects of the increased public spending also generate an excessive attraction of resources.

fiscal religion were removed, what was there to constrain the spending proclivities of politicians, and, indirectly, those of voters themselves? And predictions about governmental growth and budgetary imbalance over future years are relatively easy to make, predictions that should disturb almost any observer, regardless of ideological position.

Two means of "improvement" might suggest themselves. We may acknowledge that the fiscal policy precepts derived from Keynesian economics are not applicable in representative democracy. From this, some might go on to suggest that basic choices on macro-economic policy be taken from the decision-making power of ordinary politicians and placed in the hands of a small group of "experts," "economic technocrats," "planners," who would, presumably, be able to "fine tune" the national economy, in accordance with the true "public interest," and wholly free of political interference. This somewhat naive approach ignores the question concerning the proper incentives for the "experts," along with the demonstrated difficulties in forecasting. Furthermore, the historical record of the Federal Reserve Board, which perhaps comes closest to fitting such an institutional model, should give pause to anyone proposing reform in this direction. Nonetheless, despite such arguments, proposals for "national economic planning" surfaced again in 1975. This direction for change represents an attempt to reproduce for America the basic Keynesian presuppositions for fiscal choice.

There are, of course, strong normative objections to any such removal of decision-making power from the elected representatives of the citizens. If, for these or other reasons, the basic spending and taxing decisions are to be retained by the politicians, the economist who acknowledges the biases of the political process must reconsider his often too-ready acceptance of the Keynesian policy prescriptions. The fiscal policy that is "ideal" for the "ideal" world need not be best for the world of practical politics. This suggests that the economist who seeks to be of assistance must become a "political economist" in a very real sense. He must pay some attention to the political institutions through which any policy advice must be translated into policy actions.

Almost by necessity, the political economist who acknowledges that the biases discussed in this paper exist and are important, but who also works within the basic value precepts of representative democracy, is forced into a consideration of what may be called the "fiscal constitution," the set of constraints within which elected political representatives operate. In this perspective, the acceptance of the Keynesian paradigm, misplaced in its cognitive foundations, has led to the destruction of one important element of this constitution, an element that has not been replaced. And the spending and inflating proclivities that have been unleashed are capable of making the economy appear to conform to the Keynesian paradigm. The sophisticated replacements that have been discussed by economists, budget balance over the cycle, or budget balance at high employment, have not proved to be effective in constraining politicians. In 1976 it seems clear that explicit constitutional action is required to restore some constraint on the proclivities of politicians, and ultimately, of voters toward spending excesses.[19]

---

19. Discussion of particular reforms is not appropriate in this paper, for such discussion is the task of the paper by Niskanen. For a brief statement of some of the pertinent constitutional issues that emerge from our perspective, see James M. Buchanan and Richard E. Wagner, "Deficit Spending in Constitutional Perspective," in *Balancing the Budget*, Hearings before the Subcommittee on Constitutional Amendments, Committee of the Judiciary, United States Senate, 94th Congress, 1st Session 1975 (Washington: U. S. Government Printing Office, 1975), pp. 61–64.

Appendix

The Irrelevance of Institutional Forms:
Fiscal Choice in the Purely Ricardian World

"Institutions matter." In one sense, this is the central theme of our paper. And if our arguments in support have been convincing, little more need be added. Nonetheless, a flank has been left unprotected, and we shall, in this Appendix, examine critically the arguments that are advanced by modern-day Ricardians, who reject our central proposition, regardless of the political structure. If voters, and their political representatives, are able to see through the "fiscal illusions" that the abandonment of budget-balance creates, they should behave no differently than they would have behaved under the budget-balance constraint. There would in this case be no effects of Keynesian fiscal policy; budgetary manipulation would be of no avail. In this respect, we are with the Keynesians, not the Ricardians. The creation of budget deficits can influence aggregate spending in the economy. To this point we are Keynesian analysts. But it can also influence other decisions; it is this that our paper discusses.

David Ricardo advanced the proposition that tax finance and debt finance are basically equivalent.[20] The imposition of a tax directly reduces the net worth of the taxpayer, but the issue of an equivalent amount of government debt generates an equal reduction because of the capitalization of the future tax liabilities that are required to service and to amortize the debt. Suppose, for example, that the market rate of interest is 10 percent, and that a tax of $100 on a person is replaced by an identical share of public debt issue, with the debt obligation to be met with a payment of $110 in one year. This shift does not affect the taxpayer's net worth. This Ricardian "equivalence theorem" is little more than simple arithmetic in the choice setting of a single person, provided, of course, that the person in question has access to perfectly working capital markets, either as borrower or as lender. Such a person would remain wholly indifferent as to whether the government financed its outlay by tax or by debt since, by assumption, the present value of the fiscal liability, to him, is identical under the two alternatives, and, furthermore by assumption, he is assumed to have full knowledge of this equivalence.

To the extent that shifts among the forms of financing generate or might generate differences in the distribution of fiscal liabilities among persons and groups in the economy, the Ricardian theorem may not apply generally.[21] This difficulty can be forestalled by assuming implicitly that all persons are equal, at least in the relevant respects for this analysis. This allows us to stay within the choice setting for the single citizen.[22]

Under these restrictions, the equivalence theorem can be generalized beyond the straightforward tax-debt comparison. In its most inclusive variant, the

20. David Ricardo, *The Principles of Political Economy and Taxation, Works and Correspondence*, Vol. I, edited by P. Sraffa (Cambridge: Cambridge University Press, 1951), pp. 244–249.
21. The prospect that real-world shifts among financing instruments and specifically between tax and debt finance would generate such distributional differences provided the basis for Griziotti's attack on the Ricardian theorem. See, B. Griziotti, "La diversa pressione tributaria del prestito e dell' imposta," *Giornale degli economisti* (1917).

theorem would assert that the particular way in which government extracts resources from citizens is irrelevant in influencing either private or public choice. Tax finance may be replaced by debt finance; either may be replaced by money creation; a personal income tax may be replaced by a corporation income tax, a sales tax, or a property tax. So long as the same governmental outlay is financed in each case, and so long as this outlay is shared among individuals in the same way (in this example, equally) there are no effects of institutions on outcomes.[23] The theorem rests on the fundamental presumption that each person has perfect knowledge about how changes in the means of financing government affect his individual net worth. And if the alternatives are presented so as to ensure that the arithmetic value of the fiscal charge is identical under all institutional forms, the precepts of rationality clearly dictate indifference as among these.

We shall criticize the extreme assumptions of this theorem momentarily. The point to be noted here is that, under these strict Ricardian assumptions, the particular form in which public outlays are financed will have no effects on individual behavior, either in the private or the public sector. Voters, and the politicians who represent them, would be fully aware of the real cost of public outlays which would remain invariant regardless of financing methods. Alleged Keynesian biases could not characterize the political choice process in this purely rational, Ricardian world, although the logical bases of the precepts which dictate changes in fiscal institutions are also absent.

At a common level of consideration, the assumptions about information required by the Ricardian model seem to be absurd. Even professional economists are often unable to agree on the consequences of changes in the institutional means of extracting resources from citizens. The continuing and unresolved dispute over the incidence of the corporation income tax is but one illustration. And this inability refers to disagreement over such broad functional categories as consumer prices, factor prices, rents, and profits. Disagreement would be intensified should efforts actually be made to present specific dollar magnitudes for individual citizens. The Ricardian-like proclivity to reduce analysis to mathematical comparison is itself highly deceptive because it conceals the assumption that the taxpayer-arithmetician possesses full knowledge of all the relevant data.[24] But these data often cannot even be

22. For a modern attempt to apply the Ricardian theorem, without reference to Ricardo, see, Robert J. Barro, "Are Government Bonds Net Wealth," *Journal of Political Economy* 82 (November/December 1974): 1095–1118. For a criticism of Barro's analysis, see, James M. Buchanan, "Barro on the Ricardian Equivalence Theorem," *Journal of Political Economy* 84 (April 1976), pp. 337–342.

23. This conclusion may seem contrary to the excess-burden analysis in incidence theory and theoretical welfare economics. The assumption that the individual is to be subjected to the same fiscal charge under each institution and that he has full information about this invariance serves to remove the excess-burden setting. The excess-burden of particular taxation arises only because the individual perceives that he can, by modifying his own behavior, affect the total fiscal charge imposed upon him. In this context, the excess-burden framework is inconsistent with the Ricardian.

24. The imposition of "perfect knowledge," while convenient for many economists, generates absurdity in the visions of social order that are implied by such models. On this, see Friedrich A. Hayek, "Economics and Knowledge," *Economica* 4 (February 1937): 33–54; and "The Use of Knowledge in Society," *American Economic Review* 35 (September 1945): 519–530; both of which are reprinted in his *Individualism and Economic Order* (Chicago: University of Chicago Press, 1948), pp. 33–56 and 77–91, respectively.

estimated without first constructing some hypothesis or model for the working of the economy, and of the way in which a change in the means of financing government works its way through the economic process. In other words, in order to make inferences about his bill for government, the taxpayer must, to be fitted into the Ricardian model, be able to solve some model of the workings of the whole economic system, and be able to relate his personal position to that solution.[25]

It is the *perceptions* of individuals concerning the differential effects of fiscal institutions that are relevant to potential fiscal choice. Empirical evidence abounds to suggest that specialized professional economists are unable to agree on the consequences of many forms of financing budgets. It seems, therefore, reasonable to infer that ordinary citizens do *not* possess full knowledge as to how they may be personally affected by changes in fiscal instruments.[26]

The Ricardian framework is also one that abstracts from distributional differentials among citizens. A shift from, say, income taxation to money creation would affect different citizens differently unless such effects are explicitly ruled out by a world-of-equals assumption. Without some such assumption, the "price" of government would fall for some citizens and rise for others, changes which would, in turn, probably produce differences in the workings of the decision processes which generate budgetary outcomes.

Neither the arithmetical, and hence informational, simplicity nor the world-of-equals character of fiscal activities in the Ricardian model describes modern democratic societies. Different means of financing government convey different signals to different people, and, moreover, persons will vary in their ability to read such signals. Additionally, even if all persons possessed full knowledge, the shifts among financing instruments may not affect all persons equally. Consequently, changes in the institutional means through which government extracts resources, including the replacement of budget balance (which implies tax financing), can alter the resulting public budgetary outcomes.[27]

25. The same applies, of course, to almost any change in economic policy. This central point is emphasized by Professor Rutledge Vining in his methodological critique of modern political economy. See, for instance, Rutledge Vining, "On the Problem of Recognizing and Diagnosing Faultiness in the Observed Performance of an Economic System," *Journal of Law and Economics* 5 (October 1962): 165–184.

26. By saying that behavior depends on perceptions about underlying economic realities rather than on the objective realities themselves, we are implying that errors can be made, and that the probabilities of error may be related to the difficulties of matching perception with reality. In support of our position here, we may cite Frank H. Knight:

"If we ignore error and values, and stick to objective, physical "facts," we are no longer talking about "economics" . . . Economic behavior is more than mechanical cause and effect. Its indubitable affection by error proves that, and otherwise it should not merit a distinctive name. And subsuming it under positive phenomena would merely deny a large and undeniable realm of reality of the human problem of living and acting."

Frank H. Knight, "Introduction" to Carl Menger, *Principles of Economics.* Translated by James Dingwall and Bert Hoselitz (Glencoe: The Free Press, 1950), p. 21.

27. For a conceptual and empirical examination of the ability of tax institutions to influence the perceived price of government, thereby modifying budgetary outcomes, see Richard E. Wagner, "Revenue Structure, Fiscal Illusion, and Budgetary Choice," *Public Choice* 24 (Spring 1976), 45–61.

COMMENTS

William H. Meckling

I have a strong urge to sympathize with the views expressed by Buchanan and Wagner in their paper. It has always seemed to me that the success of the "General Theory" was largely based in ideology rather than economics. The "new economics" of the 1940s was enthusiastically embraced in the profession by those who for other reasons wanted to see the government pursue the kinds of policies which the Keynesian framework implied. Keynes lent them a respectability which they would not otherwise have had. At the same time, it is only fair to recognize that the heat with which Keynesian views have been opposed in other quarters is, at least in part, a reflection of values held by anti-Keynesians who oppose, again on other grounds, the kinds of government policies implied by the Keynesian analysis. I count myself among the latter. Nevertheless, I confess that neither the analysis of Buchanan and Wagner, nor the evidence that they or I can adduce for their main thesis, seems very convincing to me. Let me turn first to the analysis. Later I shall talk about the evidence, though in some respects, it is hard to avoid intermingling them in the discussion.

The authors have a model which I believe we can fairly summarize as containing the following propositions:

1. Politicians act in accord with the desires of voters.
2. Voters have (since 1960) generally accepted Keynesianism – in particular, they have accepted the principle of budget balancing over the "cycle" in place of the classic, more strict rule of annual budget balancing.
3. Voters characteristically approve expenditures, but oppose taxes.

The combination of these three propositions has had the following consequences:

1. more or less continuously unbalanced budgets – seldom has there been an actual surplus;
2. progressively growing deficits;
3. high rates of inflation;

4. increased growth in the relative size of government.

The authors also argue that Keynes suffered from, what we might call the "Harvey Road Syndrome." While that issue may be important in the history of economic thought, it is not essential to their positive political economics.

The paper has one major analytical problem, which the authors perceive and have attempted to deal with in an Appendix. It is a difficult, frustrating problem which continuously confronts us in economics, namely, what level of knowledge we should attribute to the individuals who form the basic units of our analysis. A "rationalist" view of the knowledge issue would have the individual equate the marginal cost of knowledge to the marginal benefit. While they never make their model explicit, that seems to me to be the view which Wagner and Buchanan take. That model has one major flaw when it is applied to voting behavior. It is hard to explain why voters "qua voters" incur *any* costs to acquire knowledge, especially about national issues, since in fact they cannot affect the outcome of any election. Indeed, it is hard to explain why they ever bother to vote. Over the years, professional economists have devoted an enormous effort to translating and clarifying Keynes. Is it reasonable to argue that rational individuals (the general public) have found it in their interest to learn enough about those issues to substitute Keynes for the strict annual budget-balancing rule which they can easily relate to their own circumstances?

Even if we could somehow get around that problem, however, Buchanan and Wagner have a serious problem of inconsistently applying the model. If I were to characterize their position in its most extreme form, it is that voters have found it in their interest to understand the "General Theory," but not to understand that there is no such thing as a free lunch. On the one hand they argue that voters have come to understand Keynesian theory:

> The acceptance of Keynesian ideas by the politicians and the general voting public is often dated from the onset of the 1960s . . . What is there about the acceptance of Keynesian economics that generates the fiscal experience witnessed in the years after 1961?

On the other hand, those same voters do not understand the consequences of federal surpluses or, what comes to the same thing, do not understand the consequences of rapidly and continuously increasing public debt.

No doubt the authors would answer that they do not mean that the general public *really* understands Keynes. But if that is the case, why is it necessary that voters *really* understand the implications of rapidly and continuously increasing public debt? Why must they meet Buchanan and Wagner's strict requirements as set forth in the quote below, for understanding surpluses?

> In order for the indirect benefits from budget surpluses to offset fully the absence of direct benefits, it would be necessary for citizens to know fully what is at stake in choosing between politicians who propose to spend the revenues that might otherwise generate a potential budget surplus and politicians who propose to generate the surplus by holding down public outlays. Citizens would have to understand how the surplus would operate in restraining inflationary forces in the aggregate, and they would also have to be able to relate this restraint to a personal level of benefit. That is, it would be necessary for citizens to interpret the aggregate economy in precisely the manner that it is interpreted by the economists (*if only they provided a single interpretation,*) as well as to develop a relation between this aggregative pattern and their own personal well-being. The very intensity of controversy among economists over precisely such matters, however, attests to the extreme unreasonableness of such requirements. Therefore, the benefits of a budgetary surplus in restraining inflation will to some extent be under-estimated by the citizenry.

The mere use of undefined terms such as "direct" and "indirect" benefits in this paragraph makes one uncomfortable, but more to the point, must the general public "fully" understand monetary theory before it decides that inflation is having adverse effects on them as individuals, and the rascals ought to be thrown out? Where is the loyal opposition? Don't they have a strong incentive to educate the general public, to blame the inflation on the deficits?

While, as I have mentioned earlier, the authors recognize the knowledge problem in an Appendix, their discussion there does not address the correct issue. In that Appendix, they argue that the "Ricardian model," which assumes perfect knowledge on the part of voters, is inappropriate in a world in which knowledge is on the one hand costly, and on the other hand, not very valuable. It is one thing to reject the "perfect knowledge" assumption, but it is another entirely different thing to make a case for any given alternative, especially an alternative which is applied inconsistently.

Let me turn now to the question of evidence. In the end, the only way we can resolve the question of the appropriate level of knowledge to attribute to voters is by looking at the evidence. In support of their position, the authors adduce three sets of facts for the period since 1961, one dealing with the growth of government, one dealing with continuing and growing deficits, and one dealing with inflation.

Between 1961 and 1976, there was only one year of budget surplus for the federal government. The 15 years of deficit totalled some $240 billion. Moreover, the annual deficits increased in magnitude over this period. For 1961–68, the cumulative deficit was $60 billion; for 1970–74, it was $67 billion, and for the two-year period, 1975–76, more than $110 billion. We observe a dramatic increase in the relative size of government over this period, accompanied by inflation unmatched in other than war periods. Total governmental expenditures increased from somewhat less than one-third of National Income (from 32.8 percent) in 1960, to a little more than two-fifths (40.4 percent) of National Income in 1974. The consumer price index rose by 92.3 percent over this same period, and accelerated more or less in step with the size of the federal deficits.

None of these facts would count as significant evidence in a serious attempt to test the Buchanan-Wagner thesis. It is not at all clear why the "General Theory" which was published in 1936, finally came to be accepted only 25 years later, but perhaps one could argue that a 25-year lag is about what one ought to expect.

The evidence the authors present for the proposition that Keynesianism is responsible for growth of government since 1961 seems to me to be least convincing of all. Much of that growth occurred at the state and local level, where it would be difficult to argue that public acceptance of the increases was in any way significantly affected by macro-economic considerations. Data which were available to me from two separate sources indicate very little growth in nominal *federal* expenditures as a fraction of nominal GNP during the last fifteen years. In one case they rose from 20 to 22 percent of GNP and in the other, from 18.3 to 21.5 percent.

Moreover, the increase in total government expenditures from 32.8 percent of National Income to 40.4 percent which they describe as dramatic, is at most, a modest deviation from a long-standing trend. Just for reassurance, I dug out an old Economics Almanac and computed the change in that statistic for six 15-year periods beginning in the years 1920 and going through 1925. On average for the 1920–25 period, government expenditures were 14 percent of National Income. Fifteen years later, that is, for the period from 1935 through 1940, government expenditures averaged 25 percent of National Income. In 1946, government expenditures were 26.6 percent of National Income compared to the 32.8 percent in 1960 which Buchanan and Wagner cite; again, the increase was not significantly different from what they report for the 1960 to 1974 period.

The inflation data and the deficits which Buchanan and Wagner cite appear to lend more credence to their views than the data on growth in government. If one believes, as I do, that the deficits are largely the cause of the inflation, these results are simply two facets of the same phenomena, not two independent sets of data. How much support do they provide for the proposition that Keynesianism has taken over? Not very much, I am afraid. If we look at them carefully, we find that it is very misleading to talk about the 1960–76 time period as a unit. From 1961 to 1970, a period which included a not inconsequential war, the total deficit was $60 billion, an average of only $6 billion per year, and $25 billion of that was concentrated in one year, 1968. In five of those ten years, the deficit was less than $4 billion. It seems surprising to me that, given the Vietnam War, we had as little growth in federal debt in that decade as actually occurred. During that same decade, the CPI went from 89.6 to 116.3, and 12 points of that were in the last two years. It is difficult for me at least to see much evidence in these facts to support the view that a one-sided form of Keynesianism was having much of an impact.

All of the really dramatic shift has occurred in this decade. For the six years 1971 through 1976, federal deficits totaled $174 billion, an average of $29 billion a year. In the five years between 1971 and the last month of 1975, the CPI rose from 121.3 to 155.4. What we have to explain is this sudden explosion. Indeed, I would argue the problem is much bigger than an examination of government spending, deficits, and inflation would suggest, for there has been a contemporaneous explosion in government's penchant for regulating almost anything and everything anyone happens to think up.

Mancur Olson*

I.

Buchanan and Wagner's paper provides an unusual and suggestive perspective on some of the most important problems of our time. Though I shall soon argue that their model is logically incomplete, and that when it is completed a significantly different story emerges, this does not deny that their paper is most intriguing and provocative. One cannot fully appreciate why the paper is so likely to stimulate interest and controversy without looking at it from the perspective of different ideologies and schools of economic thought. Normally the economist should be skeptical about any argument that dwells on ideological disputes and the competing conceptions of different "schools" of economics — these disputes and conceptions often distract attention from important scientific tasks and also may lump together very different economists who happen to have the same university affiliation or political tendency. In this particular case, however, the ideological and methodological fires seem to provide more light than we can get anywhere else.

One reason is that Buchanan and Wagner's paper is so very different in its approach from that of most of the other economists who share their classical liberal ideology. Many economists who might often be supposed to be in the same tent as Buchanan and Wagner will consider this paper profoundly heretical. Certainly the spirited discussion at the conference at which this paper was presented suggests that this will be so. Their paper has an emphasis and orientation that is utterly unlike most of the rest of the macroeconomic literature, whatever its ideological coloration.

Above all, the Buchanan-Wagner paper is utterly unlike most of the monetarist writing. Instead of telling us, as the hard-line monetarists do, that only money matters, our authors say rather that "institutions matter," and matter a great deal. If the use of some loose but still helpful designations is allowed, we can say that this paper is not of the "Chicago School," but rather of the "Virginia School," and that it nicely illustrates how profoundly these two schools, which many economists unknowingly lump

*The author thanks the National Science Foundation and the Resources for the Future for support of his research.

together, differ. This difference is evident not only from the contrast between the emphasis of this paper and that of the typical monetarist article, but also in some assumptions which are used, but unfortunately only implicitly, in the Buchanan-Wagner paper.

II.

We can see these implicit assumptions by examining the paper's central policy conclusion — that the replacement of the old belief that governments should normally have balanced budgets with the Keynesian conviction that budget deficits and surpluses ought to be used to combat depression and inflation, has led to inflation and the growth of the public sector. Blaming inflation on budget deficits is, of course, proto-typically Keynesian. Reference to this sort of causal connection was anything but common among leading economists before Keynes. As we all know, monetarists explain inflation in terms of increases in the quantity of money, and bring in budget deficits and fiscal policy only if, and to the extent that, monetary authorities choose to combine them with changes in the stock of money. Admittedly, in their more recent book-length discussion of this topic,[1] Buchanan and Wagner recognize that "there are economists who would deny that deficits are inflationary" and go on to pacify such economists by asserting that existing monetary institutions will tend to bring about monetary expansion when there are budget deficits. One does not need to question this assertion to demonstrate the nonmonetarist character of Buchanan and Wagner's main policy conclusion. If increases in the stock of money are the only cause of inflation, the link between these increases and budget deficits ought to have been documented with a good deal of empirical evidence and explained in theoretical terms as well. Moreover, if budget deficits lead to inflation only because authorities choose to link them to increases in the money supply, then Buchanan and Wagner have to explain why the authorities maintain such a linkage. Though the high levels of output and employment that may co-exist with inflation are politically popular, inflation *per se* is patently and almost universally

1. *Democracy in Deficit: The Political Legacy of Lord Keynes* (New York: Academic Press, 1977), pp. 58–59.

unpopular. Thus, if both the monetarist argument and the Buchanan-Wagner assumption that political leaders maximize chances of re-election are true, we should expect to see politicians preventing inflation through monetary policy at the same time as they run up budget deficits. To their credit, Buchanan and Wagner make the important and, I think, probably correct point that our institutions have a bias toward budget deficits and tight money. But if the monetarist argument is altogether true, why doesn't the money supply get tightened to the point where there is no inflation? If Buchanan and Wagner were to reply that political leaders didn't understand that inflation is due to increases in the quantity of money, they would still be in trouble, for if *this* lack of understanding is the source of inflation, then the political bias in favor of budget deficits that worries them so need have nothing to do with inflation. Thus I conclude that if (as I suspect) there is some basis for their fear that the political incentives for budget deficits must be inflationary, then that can be so only because there is at least a germ of truth in the Keynesian model.

III.

A similar problem emerges when we ask *why* the politicians have the hypothesized incentive to create inflation. Obviously taxes are unpopular, and that fact should push the politicians toward deficit financing, but inflation is unpopular too, and that fact should push them toward budget surpluses. Thus the Buchanan-Wagner conclusion that the political incentives provide an inflationary bias can be justified only by a demonstration that the inflation resulting from a deficit will be less costly to the politicians or the voters than the taxes or reduced public spending that would have prevented that inflation would have been. On this point the paper under discussion is much too reticent, and even the book leaves something to be desired. In the book, Buchanan and Wagner refer to alleged psychological and informational asymmetries between the costs of extra taxation (or lower public spending) and those of inflation. There may very well be such asymmetries, but that has by no means been established, and even if it had there would be grave questions about whether these asymmetries would be sufficient to explain more than a fraction of the inflation that Buchanan and Wagner attribute to the passing of the belief in balanced budgets. The frailty of this link in the chain of argument that leads to their conclusion can readily be illustrated. In their book[2] they say that

> the direct consequences of the [budget] surplus take the form of reductions in *presently enjoyed* consumption. If taxes are raised, the consumption of private services is reduced; if expenditures are reduced, the consumption of public services is reduced. In either case, the policy of budget surplus requires citizens to sacrifice services that they are presently consuming.
>
> The indirect consequences, on the other hand, are of an altogether different nature psychologically. The benefit side of the surplus policy is never experienced, but rather must be *creatively imagined* (All italics theirs).

It would be unfair to accuse economists as capable as Buchanan and Wagner of having made the howling error that this passage read by itself seems to contain, but it is surely altogether fair to say that the exposition here is somewhat misleading and that the argument is moreover far from sufficient to bear all the weight that is put upon it. Without pretending for a moment that Buchanan and Wagner don't know this, one must still point out here that any budget surplus that is needed to prevent inflation (at least in their world where the level of unemployment and real output is not supposed to be increased by inflation) can be obtained without reducing either real private consumption or the real value of government services in the slightest. The expansionary fiscal policies that so worry Buchanan and Wagner can bring about inflation only by creating a level of aggregate effective demand for more output than the economy can produce, so that aggregative equilibrium can be re-established only at a higher price level. Any budget surplus or fiscal policy needed to prevent this inflation need only constrain aggregate demand to the point where it will be just sufficient to purchase the full employment output of the economy at present prices: the society will have just as much real output (indeed, if inflation has an "excess burden," even more) to consume with an ideal anti-inflationary fiscal policy as it would have with an inflationary fiscal policy, so an anti-inflationary policy need involve no "reduction in *presently enjoyed* consumption" as compared with an inflationary fiscal policy. To be sure, if the Phillips curve has the non-vertical slope that Buchanan and Wagner elsewhere deny, so that inflation creates extra real output, then the foregoing criticism doesn't hold, but in that case it is by no means obvious that the inflation they complain about is on balance undesirable.

2. *Ibid.*, p. 100.

Buchanan and Wagner probably intended to convey the impression that an individual who faced higher tax rates because of a countercyclical budget surplus, yet somehow assumed that the economy would not be affected by the tax increase and the budget surplus that resulted from it, would imagine that the tax increase needed to prevent inflation would leave him worse off than he would have been had the tax rates not been increased. It is entirely possible that some people will think in that way, but when the point is stated in the way I have just stated it, it is by no means obvious that most voters find anti-inflationary fiscal policies so much more objectionable psychologically than the alternative of inflation, that this possible psychological asymmetry could explain the extraordinary amount of inflation that Buchanan and Wagner purport to explain.

What has just been said does not by any means necessarily invalidate the Buchanan-Wagner conclusions, but it does strongly suggest that their argument cannot be accepted as a complete and satisfactory explanation unless additional evidence, or reasons why voters would choose inflationary policies over stabilizing ones, is provided.

IV.

An additional reason why political leaders might find somewhat inflationary fiscal policies more attractive than stabilizing ones, even under the assumption that the aggregate level of real output is in the long run independent of the level of aggregate demand, can be found if we look more closely at an aspect of the society's social decision processes that Buchanan and Wagner have ignored. Though the new political economy or public choice methods that Buchanan and Wagner use are commonly applied only to governments, they are obviously also applicable to non-governmental organizations as well. Clearly there are many collectivities besides governments that must decide what choices to make, such as labor unions, cartels, corporations, clubs, and even families and informally organized collusive groupings. In some cases, such as the sub-set of perfectly competitive firms that earn little or no rents, the entity has few if any important options: if it chooses, say, any factor mix or level of output other than the profit maximizing one it may be forced out of business, so that the collective decision in any board of directors it has becomes less important. There are of course a great many firms, both in perfectly competitive industries and also where monopoly is present, that earn rents (or profits that may not yet have been capitalized into rents). In these cases, it is possible that the firms can make several different choices about factor use or levels of output and price, each of which choices may be consistent for a time with survival. Labor unions, professional associations, and any combinations of firms that control entry have an even clearer area of discretion. Most labor unions, for example, can choose among at least a narrow range of different wage levels. To be sure (unless there is monopsony), higher wages must mean lower levels of employment[3] but the union can often choose a number of different points on the marginal revenue product of labor or demand for labor curves of the firms with which they deal. This means that there are some units in the economy that can choose a particular wage or price, and hold to that wage or price without losing their viability, even if the economy changes and makes the price or wage nonoptimal.

Now consider the subset of these rent-earning entities that are themselves collectivities and must therefore be hosts to some meaningful collective decision process. Think of the unions that must decide for each contract period how to trade-off higher wages versus a lower quantity of labor demanded, or the professional associations that effectively determine how many can enter a given profession, or the regulated companies that can influence their regulators and must decide how to use the protected entry their public utility status gives them. In such cases as these the individual members of the union, or the individual members of any other such combination, have their own distinct individual interests. The senior workers who won't be laid off may have an interest in much higher wages, whereas the junior workers who might be laid off may want only such wage increases as are consistent with maintaining the present level of employment. In each of these cases there must be some bargaining or other collective decision process which derives a single policy for the whole collectivity out of the diverse and in some degree conflicting interests of each of the individual participants.

3. In a general equilibrium setting there is a qualification to this assertion which is, however, of little practical importance here.

These collective choice processes may procede very slowly. Elections may be held only periodically or boards of directors may meet only periodically. Since it is often rational for a participant in a bargaining process to threaten to hold out from any bargain unless he gets better terms, sometimes even when such a threat is not sincere, bargaining can take a very long while. This means that some of the wage rates in the economy, and even on occasion a few of the prices, will remain fixed for a time, even though the economy meanwhile has changed in a way that makes them nonoptimal for the entity that chose them. Similarly, they may change on occasion if the economic environment has not changed, simply because some collective decision process has finally produced a new decision.

When the obvious costs of changing price or wage schedules for some firms (e.g., those that have large catalogues), even if they are not host to any collective decision process, and the prevalence of long term contracts, are added, we see that many wages and prices in the economy will change only slowly, even if there are distinct changes in economic environment of the entities that set or influence these wages and prices. Of course, the idea that some wages and prices are "sticky" is hardly novel. The point needs making here, though, because some of this rigidity is due to collective decision processes of the kind Buchanan and Wagner emphasize, and also because this fact helps us make their argument complete.

What Buchanan and Wagner have above all left out is the fact that many wages and prices are rather sticky. The existence of any such rigidities can affect what Milton Friedman and many other monetarists would call the "natural rate of unemployment," or in a period of falling aggregate demand create what Keynesians would call involuntary unemployment. They can also help to explain what we see again and again in the United States as well as many other countries: a correlation between increases in aggregate demand and increases in the level of real output. The political leader who arranges for an inflationary budget deficit is very likely indeed to find that in the short run the result of this is a higher level of output. Demand for output rises, but some wages and prices do not change for a time. Most notably, some wages, set in money terms by a collective decision process that channot change things quickly, fall in real terms. With lower real wages in some lines, some employers hire more workers, so the unemployment rate falls, the real value of output rises, and for a time most people are indeed probably better off.

In the long run, to be sure, wage and price levels will adjust to the inflationary expansion of demand, and society may end up with more inflation and no enduring increase in real output. But our political leaders are elected for terms of only two, four, or six years. By the time the inflation arrives it may be some other politician's problem, and in any event the politician at issue has maximized his chances of getting through the next election.

This asymmetry in the lags between the good and the bad consequences of an inflationary budget-deficit in my judgment is one of the most important elements needed to complete the Buchanan and Wagner argument. With the asymmetry in lags, due in large part to collective decision processes not unlike the ones students of public choice are used to talking about, we have at least a partial answer to the question of why politicians often find inflationary deficits preferable to stabilizing fiscal policies. It is probably not that the voters are less opposed to inflation than to the tax rates that would give them the same level of real output plus stable prices; it is rather that the inflation comes later, perhaps in someone else's term, whereas the benefits of the deficit are available now. This type of explanation is, of course, exactly what the undefinitive but still substantial evidence in favor of a political business cycle should have led us to look for.

V.

The notoriously high discount rates of most elected officials, which Niskanen has perhaps emphasized the most strongly, give us a good reason to look for other real or imagined lags which might affect the rate of inflation or the size of the public sector. Interestingly enough, there is one really striking change in perceived lag structure which Buchanan and Wagner emphasize, but which they do not for some reason put in the usual public choice framework with its victory-maximizing politicians and rational, self-interested voters. This was the change in the perceived lag between the costs and benefits that occurred when the conversion from the classical conception of public debt, with its emphasis on the fact that a society which financed its current consumption expenditures by borrowing was leaving a burden for future periods or generations, to the modern or Keynesian theory, which argues that the resources used up by a government that engages in deficit spending are withdrawn from current alternative uses (or from unemployment, if there is a depression), so that there need be no burden for future generations.

Under the old or classical theory of public debt, the politician anxious to attain or maintain power would attract support from his constituents by financing some of his expenditure out of borrowings. If we accept Buchanan and Wagner's premise that the classical theory of debt was generally accepted in the pre-Keynesian days, those among the politician's constituents who valued the utility of their heirs less than their own, or who had no heirs, would necessarily choose (if they were rational and self-interested) to pass some of the burdens of government on to future generations. Those who valued the utility of successive generations as the equal of their own would in general be indifferent, unless the process had been carried so far that they believed their descendants would have lower post-tax incomes than themselves and thus probably a higher marginal utility of income. The net result would be political support for passing some of the burden of current expenditures on to future generations. It appears on cursory examination that there were many years and many jurisdictions around the world where this sort of process, or something very like it, actually occurred; many jurisdictions in different parts of the world had apparently accumulated debts well in excess of the value of any capital goods their governments had accumulated. Buchanan and Wagner describe such expenditures as "unconstitutional" in terms of the prevailing beliefs of the time. Though it was (and is) unconstitutional for various subordinate governments to borrow money, at least for current consumption, this was surely true only of a subset of jurisdictions. The notion of a sociological or religious attitude that is akin to a constitution, which Buchanan and Wagner introduce without elaboration, would apply to other governments as well, but it is difficult indeed to see how such "constitutions" would be enforced in large pluralistic societies, or how they could have been operational, much less sufficient to control governmental behavior. So the conclusion must be that the classical theory of public debt, to the extent it was believed, must have made public indebtedness greater than it would otherwise have been.

Under the Keynesian conception of the public debt the emphasis is on the fact that the generation that engages in the deficit financing withdraws the resources it obtains in this way from any other uses the resources had at the time of the deficit spending, so that the current generation bears any burden arising from the debt. To the extent that this Keynesian conception of debt burdens is believed, the politicians and voters have no incentive to increase public sector spending in the expectation other generations will bear the costs. Thus a public choice analysis shows that the Keynesian theory of the burden of the debt should not, by itself, lead to any nonoptimal spending of borrowed money, whereas the classical theory would have exactly this effect. This is of course the opposite of the conclusion that Buchanan and Wagner draw from their sociological references to apparent or postulated variations in ethical precepts about public debt in different periods.

The foregoing argument is not in any way contradicted by the extent or number of budget deficits in the post-Keynesian period. A change in the understanding of who bears the burden of public expenditures was only one of several features of the Keynesian revolution. The feature of this pervasive change in thinking which has presumably done the most to increase deficit spending is the conclusion that such spending can bring full employment. This conclusion (whether right or wrong) has surely brought about deficit spending that would not have occurred in its absence. To the extent, as argued earlier, that demand expansion in many cases brings additional output initially, and inflation only later, deficit spending will be further encouraged. (In a more detailed analysis, a distinction should be made between *ex ante* and early-period deficits and any *ex post* or end-of-period deficits, to take account of the effects of any increase in money income and tax collections, but the conclusion that the Keynesian belief in obtaining full employment by deficit spending, along with the high discount rates of elected officials, have increased public debt, would presumably still hold true.) It is accordingly important to distinguish Buchanan and Wagner's belief that Keynesian ideas in general add to deficit spending (which is quite reasonable) from their judgment that the Keynesian conception of the *burdens* of public debt has added to public indebtedness (which is inconsistent with the customary public-choice assumptions used in other parts of their argument).

VI.

If what has been said so far in this comment is to a sufficient degree accepted, it follows that we have a series of possible deletions and additions to Buchanan and Wagner's argument which could make it possible to realize what this commentator believes is its true potential. There is a great deal to be said in favor of the Buchanan-Wagner concern about a political bias in the direction of inflation and a bigger public sector. There is no doubt at all that they are dead right in thinking that "institutions matter," and that there is an urgent need for more economists to take them into account. But we must replace some links and add others before the chain of their argument will reach to and carry the weight of their conclusions.

We must first of all pull out the ribbon of doctrinal monetarism that decorates their argument, but adds nothing to its strength. There is no way that the Keynesian analysis of fiscal policy could have *as much* significance as Buchanan and Wagner attach to it if "only money matters." It is no wonder that some of the more devout monetarists have been bothered by their argument. Nor is it surprising that the scattered passages in the Buchanan-Wagner book which explain or commend the monetarist position lack the strength and lustre of their emphasis on the importance of institutions. At least some small degree of Keynesianism is essential to their argument, and this should be made explicit (though there is no reason to accept the excesses of some of Keynes apostles or to ignore the many advances in macroeconomic or monetary thought since his day).

Since inflation *per se* is patently unpopular, a link must also be added to their argument to explain why politicians do not more often avoid it. The suggestion in this comment was that this link should be constructed in large part out of the tools of the new political economy that Buchanan and Wagner and Buchanan's other colleagues and students have done so much to develop. The collective choice processes in labor unions and occasionally also in other collectivities in the private sector make many wage and price levels very sticky, and some other factors, like catalogue costs and long-term contracts, also have this effect. This stickiness, as we argued above, can make inflationary deficit-spending politically attractive over the short time horizons that are relevant to elected officials.

Finally, the by now rather rusty baling wire that Buchanan has used in prior writings about the burden of the public debt should be cut out altogether. It merely weighs down the chain of argument and thereby reduces its strength. In so far as the Keynesian conception of the burden of public debt has any relevance at all, it goes in the opposite direction from the one in which Buchanan and Wagner are pulling.

So, I submit, with these deletions and additions (plus some others involving especially floating exchange rates that it would take too long to forge now) we could have a strong chain of argument that would hold up Buchanan and Wagner's best conclusions, however many critics might try to pull them down. The chain would be made of links made by men of very different ideologies, notably by the later, reform-minded Keynes as well as by the classically liberal Buchanan and Wagner. But liberals, whether of the classical or modern variety, should not be surprised at this, for they have long believed that truth is most likely to be found through the free competition and collaboration of those with different ideologies and interests.

6. CONGRESSIONAL BUDGET REFORM: NEW DECISION STRUCTURES

Jesse Burkhead and Charles Knerr*

> What has led to this strange impairment of the power of the purse? Why has Congress, inheritor of the right wrested from the king to control national expenditure, become seemingly unable to control it, not as against King or President, but as against itself?
>
> (Rollo Ogden, "The Rationale of Congressional Extravagance," *Yale Review*, May 1897, p. 39).

Last December the U. S. Congress finished the first year's trial run of new budgetary procedures required by the Congressional Budget and Impoundment Control Act of 1974. Senator Muskie, Chairman of the Senate Budget Committee reported that the new process ". . . has so far succeeded beyond our most optimistic expectations."[1]

This year Congress faces the test: can the acclaimed success of last year's effort be made truly operational – can this complex legislation bring a larger measure of "rationality" into federal budget procedures?

Obviously it is a bit early to attempt more than preliminary judgments. The footing would be more secure if this paper were to be written two or three years hence. A sense of uneasiness will thus pervade some of these observations.

The effort here will be divided into three parts. The first will examine the background of the legislation and sketch the nature of

*For comments and conversations the authors are indebted to Allen Schick, Charles Mohan, Richard Fenno, Jerry Miner, George Schaefer, Anthony Carnevale, Calude Seguin, Roy Bahl, William Schuerch, Charles Schultz, James Sundquist, Sam Cohn, Robert Reischauer, Charles Leonard and Thomas Lynch.
1. *New York Times*, December 13, 1975, p. 44.

the reforms. The second part of this paper will be devoted to the search for a paradigm — how does this legislation fit, if at all, into prevailing fiscal theory. The final section will attempt some analysis of both the economic and political power implications of the new procedures and make some attempt at prognosis.

6.1. Retrospective

If the federal budget is indeed "out of control" — a debatable point that is examined below — this is not a mere procedural fault but is deeply imbedded in the diffusion of power characteristic of our constitutional system of checks and balances.[2] In the federal budgetary process, once the budget leaves the hands of the President there is no longer any possibility for central decision-making. The President does not defend the budget in the Congress. OMB may present testimony in an overview before the Joint Economic Committee, but that Committee is far removed from the appropriations process. OMB may also send representatives for overview statements to Appropriations Committee hearings but the defense of budget requests is the primary responsibility of department heads, their budget officers and bureau and agency chiefs.

The Diffusion of Authority

The committee structure of the Congress presides over the diffusion of authority. Not only is revenue authority divided from expenditure authority, but expenditure authority — authorizations to incur obligations — is divided among the subcommittees of the House Appropriations Committee with the Senate Appropriations Committee exercising a kind of appellate role. This state of affairs appears to be largely inevitable in a nation dedicated to political pluralism.

The year 1921 is the landmark in the chronicles of Presidential-Congressional struggle for control of the federal government's purse

2. Foreign observers have often commented on this point — de Toqueville and James Bryce, for example. A more recent critic is Andrew Shonfield, *Modern Capitalism* (New York: Oxford University Press, 1969), pp. 298–357.

strings. During the first one hundred thirty-four years of federal budget making, the Congress held virtually undisputed control over taxes and expenditures. During this period, Article 1, Section 9 of the Constitution was interpreted quite literally:

> No money shall be drawn from the treasury, but in consequence of appropriations made by law.

With the enactment of the Budget and Accounting Act of 1921 the Congress began a long process of ceding control to the Executive. The Act provided an avenue for increasingly centralized coordination of budget-making, with control and coordination centered in the Executive Office of the president after 1939.

After World War II the Congress attempted to reassert its budgetary role by reducing the traditional diffusion of legislative fiscal authority. The Legislative Reorganization Act of 1946 established a Joint Committee on the Legislative Budget, with responsibility for setting appropriation and expenditure ceilings by concurrent resolution. This was abandoned after two years' experience. In 1950 the House Appropriations Committee experimented with an Omnibus Appropriations Bill, but this was strenuously opposed by the chairmen of the sub-committees and was abandoned. During the 1950s there were numerous proposals for a Joint Committee on the Budget. These were typically supported by the Senate and opposed by the House.[3]

During the late 1960s and early 1970s the Congress attempted to modify the budget process by enacting annual spending ceilings. Ceilings were considered each year beginning in 1968. Although in three years ceilings were actually set, these attempts failed, for a variety of reasons.[4]

During this 30-year period of unsuccessful experiments and continued concern over Congressional budget reform there were other factors at work. Appropriation bills came to be more and more delayed; the new fiscal year would sometimes be more than half completed before the Congress could finish its authorizations.[5] The Congress came to feel increasingly impotent in its budgetary

3. For a history of these efforts see Jesse Burkhead, *Government Budgeting* (New York: Wiley & Sons, 1956), pp. 326–339.
4. For a review of these efforts, see Joel Havemann, "Budget Report/Ford, Congress Seek Handle on 'Uncontrollable Spending,'" *National Journal* 6:48 (November 29, 1975), pp. 1619–1626.

control as "backdoor spending" (discussed below) grew prominent by way of borrowing authority, contract authority, permanent appropriations and entitlements.

These frustrations were accentuated by the atmosphere of Watergate, strong Congressional reaction against the Imperial Presidency and most specifically by President Nixon's impoundments in 1972 and 1973. This was the precipitating issue.[6]

President Nixon stated, at a press conference in January 1973:

> The constitutional power for the President of the United States to impound funds . . . is absolutely clear.[7]

But impoundments were viewed by the Congress as tantamount to an item veto, which is not within the scope of Presidential authority. The judiciary subsequently agreed with the Congress; the Administration has lost more than 40 cases on impoundment.[8] And underlying all of these historical and proximate factors was the current concern, shared by the Administration, the Congress and the citizenry, in various degrees, over the long term growth in the size of the federal sector.

The only rational basis for this concern must rest on fears for the future, not on the record of the recent past. As the Brookings *Priorities* volume states:

> . . . although there are many possible ways of measuring the growth of the federal sector, by most measures there has been relatively little change in the share of total output consumed by the federal government in the past sixteen

---

5. As far as can be ascertained the Congress has not been able to complete action on all appropriation bills before the beginning of the fiscal year since FY 1949.

6. James P. Pfiffner, "Congressional Budget Reform, 1974: Initiative and Reaction," paper presented to the American Political Science Association, September 1975 (mimeo).

7. *Weekly Compilation of Presidential Documents* 9:5, February 5, 1975.

8. The controlling decision is by the Supreme Court, February 1975:

> "We cannot believe that Congress . . . scuttled the entire effort by providing the Executive Branch with the seemingly limitless power to withhold funds from allotment and obligation. Yet such was the Government's position in the lower courts — combined with the argument that the discretion conferred is unreviewable."
>
> Train v. City of New York, 43
> L. W. 4209 at 4210–4211

See also, Timothy J. Gratz, "Constitutional Law-Impoundment-Separation of Powers," *Wisconsin Law Review* 1975:1, pp. 203–230; Louis Fisher, *Presidential Spending Power* (Princeton: Princeton University Press, 1975) pp. 147–201.

years . . . it would be misleading to characterize the past sixteen years as an era when the federal government took over the economy. The U. S. private sector is still alive and well.[9]

The recent growth of government in this country, as is commonly known, has been state-local growth. In this sector taxation from own resources was 9.3 percent of GNP in FY 1961, 12.3 percent in FY 1973 and will probably be 14 percent in FY 1976.

The Congress did not move hastily with reform. During the summer of 1972 President Nixon demanded a $250 billion spending ceiling for FY 1973. Both houses of Congress responded with proposed legislation limiting total spending to the level demanded by the President. After days of debate and disagreement the ceiling was rejected. An important agreement was reached, however, to establish a special joint committee to study the federal budgetary process and to recommend reform.[10] The Joint Study Committee on Budget Control would later conduct extensive hearings, and file two reports proposing a series of reforms, many of which were incorporated into the final version of the 1974 Act.[11] During the spring and fall of 1973, hundreds of bills and amendments to bills related to budgeting were introduced in both houses. Final agreement was reached during the spring of 1974. The vote on the compromise version suggests the diversity of views represented and the widespread appeal for reform. The House voted 401-6 and the Senate 75-0.[12]

It may be noted that the provision in the legislation for Congressional overview of both revenue and expenditure had been advocated for many years by students of the budgetary process — Smithies, the Committee for Economic Development, R. A. Wallace and Niskanen, among others.[13]

---

9. Barry M. Blechman, Edward M. Gramlich, Robert W. Hartmen , *Setting National Priorities: The 1976 Budget* (Washington: The Brookings Institution, 1975), p. 7. For example in FY 1961 budget outlays were 19.3 percent of GNP. In FY 1974 they were 19.8 percent; in FY 1975 22.5 percent and for FY 1976 they are estimated at 23.4 percent of GNP. Budget receipts were 18.5 percent of GNP in FY 1961 and are estimated to be 18.7 percent of GNP in FY 1976. Projections will be examined in the third section of this paper.
10. P. L. 92–599 (October 27, 1972).
11. U. S. Congress, Joint Study Committee on Budget Control, *Recommendations for Improving Control Over Budgetary Outlays and Receipt Totals*, H. Report 93–13 (February 7, 1973) and H. Report 93–147 (April 18, 1973) Government Printing Office, 1973.
12. P. L. 93–344.

The Character of the Reform

The Congressional Budget and Impoundment Control Act (hereafter CBICA) significantly alters Congressional budgetary procedures and executive-legislative budgetary relations.

Three new Congressional institutions were created by the Act: the Congressional Budget Office (CBO) and a Budget Committee in each house of Congress. The CBO was established as the principal information and analytic arm of the Congress on budgetary matters. The Budget Committees have nearly identical jurisdictions: they are charged with developing targets for fiscal policy and with recommending priorities among specified functional expenditure categories.

The Act prescribes two dates by which Congress must vote on the budget as a whole and on budgetary priorities – through the adoption of two concurrent resolutions. All other facets of the Congressional budgetary process are regulated by the outcomes of these two votes.

The first concurrent resolution on the budget, which must be adopted on or before May 15th of each year, establishes tentative targets for the forthcoming fiscal year for total budgetary authority and outlays, revenues, and the resulting surplus or deficit. The resolution must also specify target ceilings for each of sixteen functional spending categories. Targets are agreed upon through a complex deliberative process involving the Budget Committees, the Joint Economic Committee, and the various legislative committees, supported by analyses of the President's budget and projected economic conditions.

Shortly after the adoption of the first concurrent budget resolution, on or before each May 15th, the target amounts in each of the functional categories are required to be allocated among the committees of the House and Senate. Each committee must, in turn, further subdivide its allocation among subcommittees or

13. Arthur Smithies, *The Budgetary Process in the United States* (New York: McGraw Hill, 1955), pp. 192–197; CED, *Control of Federal Government Expenditures* (Washington, 1955), pp. 25–28; Robert Ash Wallace, *Congressional Control of Federal Spending* (Detroit: Wayne University Press, 1960), pp. 168–176; William A. Niskanen, *Structural Reform of the Federal Budget Process* (Washington: American Enterprise Institute, 1973). An interesting proposal to avoid legislative financial schizophrenia is suggested by Martin Bronfenbrenner, "A Percentage Budget for Public Appropriations," *National Tax Journal* 18 (December 1965), pp. 375–379.

programs, and report such subdivisions to the House and Senate. Further subdivisions are to be made between controllable and other authorizations.

The first concurrent budget resolution is intended to serve as a guide to the various committees undertaking activities on authorizations, appropriations or tax bills. Binding ceilings on expenditures and a floor for revenues are set in the second resolution, which must be adopted before September 15th of each year. Individual actions that exceed the ceilings or the floor must be changed, or the ceiling or floor modified, during reconciliation, which must be completed by September 25th of each year. Congress may not adjourn *sine die* until this reconciliation process is completed.

Once a second budget resolution has been adopted, no expenditure or tax bill may be approved which violates the levels set by the resolution. Individual expenditure ceilings or the revenue floor can be changed only by the adoption of a new concurrent budget resolution.

The Act also prescribes a timetable for other Congressional actions on the budget. Authorization bills must be reported by May 15th of each year, the date of final action on the first concurrent resolution. This authorization deadline is intended to accelerate the authorization process, and to accelerate the consideration of appropriation measures. Special exemptions are made in the Act and a waiver procedure is available in the Senate for emergency or unforeseen activities.

New appropriations, debt limit, or revenue changes may not be considered by either House until after May 15th, or after the first budget resolution is adopted. Appropriation measures are to be completed by the seventh day after Labor Day. This deadline is perhaps the most critical date in the entire process, since the second concurrent resolution must be adopted September 15th and the reconciliation by September 25th, with the fiscal year beginning October 1. Appropriation measures need to be virtually completed by the end of July, since the Congress traditionally recesses during August.

With the new fiscal year beginning in October 1976 a special transition period — July 1 to September 30 — is specified, which belongs to neither FY 76 or FY 77. The revision of the fiscal year allows the Congress additional time to act on the President's budget proposals.

Numerous new budgetary documents and reports are required by the Act. A "Current Services Budget" projecting outlays and budget authority for the forthcoming fiscal year for existing programs and other activities, is to be prepared by the President and submitted to the Congress by November 10th of each year. The Joint Economic Committee is required to analyze this document and submit a report to the Congressional Budget Committees by December 31st of each year.

The President's proposed detailed budget document must be submitted within fifteen days after Congress convenes each January. All Congressional standing and joint committees are required to analyze the proposals and report to the Budget Committees by March 15th. This includes the Joint Economic Committee and the Joint Committee on Internal Revenue Taxation. The CBO is required to analyze and report to the Budget Committees by April 1st. The President's budget is required to be updated by April 10th to include all changes after the January submission. The Budget Committees, after conducting hearings and completing their analyses of the President's original and revised proposals, must submit a report to the Congress by April 15th, recommending the tentative ceilings for the first concurrent budget resolution.

After adoption of this resolution and allocation of the functional category targets to the various Congressional Committees, the CBO is required to submit periodic "scorekeeping" reports. The CBO must also analyze reported public bills as necessary, and all bills containing new budget authority or entitlements, and tax expenditure bills, for immediate cost and five-year projections. The Budget Committees may also issue reports on these matters. On July 10th of each year the President is required to submit a revised budget proposal — an updated mid-year budget. Other than the impoundment reports (see below) there is one other report. After Congress enacts the second concurrent budget resolution, the CBO must submit a five-year cost projection of the entire budget as adopted by the Congress.

CBICA prescribes new procedures for "backdoor spending" — a term applied to funding not subject to regular appropriation processes. Legislation providing for new contract and/or borrowing authority must contain a provision that the amount of such authority will be determined through regular appropriations.[14]

14. The Budget Committees agreed to make this provision effective on March 3, 1975, pursuant to the early implementation authority provided by the Act.

Entitlement legislation, on the other hand, cannot be effective before the start of a new fiscal year, making such legislation subject to the second concurrent budget resolution and the reconciliation process. Moreover, entitlements in excess of the most recently adopted budget resolution must be referred to the Appropriations Committees. Prior to floor consideration action may be taken to reduce the entitlement level.

Certain "backdoor spending" activities are specifically exempt, including all contract or borrowing authority in effect prior to January 1975. In addition, and more importantly, exemptions are made for the social security trust funds, all ninety percent self-financed trust funds and the contract and borrowing authority of certain government corporations.

Title X of the Act governs proposed impoundment actions of the President. Two types of impoundments are defined and different processes specified for each.

Rescissions are defined as permanent reductions in budget authority for a given fiscal year. In order to become effective, a proposed rescission must be approved by the Congress within forty-five days after submission by the President. Should no action be taken, the budget authority must be made available for obligation.

Deferrals, on the other hand, are defined as temporary reductions in budget authority for a given fiscal year. A deferral remains in effect unless it is disapproved by either house. Should either house vote to disapprove a deferral the funds must be released by the President.

Rescission and deferral proposals and monthly summaries must be reported to the Congress and published in the *Federal Register*. The Comptroller General must review each message and make recommendations to the Congress. The Comptroller is also required to report any impoundments which have not been reported to the Congress. If budget authority is not made available after the Congress acts, the Comptroller is authorized to initiate a civil suit to bring about compliance.

There are a number of miscellaneous budgetary provisions. Congressional committees are authorized to conduct program review, evaluation, and other studies. Title VIII of the Act directs the General Accounting Office to cooperatively develop standardized budgetary terminology, definitions, and classifications.

Finally, new reporting requirements are specified for the President's detailed budget proposal.

The obvious conclusion is that CBICA is a most complex piece of legislation. The Congress will be provided with a vastly increased quantity (and probably quality) of budgetary data and analysis. The timetable is tight — even with the extension of the fiscal year. There are significant alternations in the distribution of spending and taxing authority within the Congress and between the Congress and the Executive.

6.2. Fiscal Theory and Decision Structures

It could hardly be expected that a major reform in federal budgetary decision structures would be explicitly predicated on academic fiscal theory. One would not expect to find, in committee reports on CBICA, explicit reference to the writings of Wicksell, Lindahl, Samuelson, Musgrave, Buchanan, Lindblom or Wildavsky. Nonetheless, it may be useful to inquire how this reform would be viewed by prevailing theories of collective choice.

There are four such theories extant, and each of these will be examined very briefly. They are: (1) the neo-classical, (2) incrementalism, (3) neo-Marxism, (4) public choice.[15]

Neo-Classical

Neo-classical fiscal theory is currently associated with public goods theory and in its contemporary versions is dated from the Samuelson articles of 1954 and 1955 and Musgrave's major contribution.[16] The fascinating and intricate problems associated with public goods that are produced under demand conditions of non-rivalry and non-exclusion are not particularly germane to an appraisal of CBICA, but Musgrave's division of the public household

---

15. This taxonomy, with the exception of neo-Marxism, is further explicated in Jesse Burkhead and Jerry Miner, *Public Expenditure* (Chicago: Aldine, 1971), Chapters 1, 5.
16. Paul A. Samuelson, "The Pure Theory of Public Expenditures," *Review of Economics and Statistics* 36 (November 1954), pp. 387–389; "Diagrammatic Exposition of a Theory of Public Expenditures," *Review of Economics and Statistics* 37 (November 1955), pp. 350–356; Richard A. Musgrave, *The Theory of Public Finance* (New York: McGraw Hill, 1959).

into three branches — distribution, stabilization and allocation — is relevant.

The responsibilities of Musgrave's mythical branch managers may be recited briefly. Income distribution is exogenously determined in accordance with Wicksellian principles of what the community views as "proper" and "just".[17] Stabilization goals are similarly exogenous; some kind of societal consensus is reached as to an appropriate rate of unemployment and presumably an appropriate rate of inflation. The allocations branch manager then reads the preferences of the citizenry for public vs. private goods, and for the composition of public outlays. Public goods are conceptualized as final output, not as intermediate goods. Taxes for the allocations branch are levied on a benefit basis. The three mythical branch managers consolidate their sub-budgets.

In this conceptual framework bureaucrats and legislators are faceless. They are not utility maximizers. It is their responsibility to read the preferences of sovereign consumers in an attempt to achieve Pareto optimality in resource allocation. And, as is well known, the central difficulty is the absence of a mechanism for preference revelation. In the neo-classical approach, for public as for private goods, unless distribution is separated from allocation, and unless preferences are revealed we must invoke that magnificently vague construct, the social welfare function, to conceptualize an optimum.

In this rarified atmosphere of neo-classical theory no attention is directed to fiscal politics or fiscal sociology or to the institutional framework of which real-world budget decisions are made. The only evident analog to the decision structures established by CBICA is that the Congress now becomes the mythical manager that consolidates stabilization, allocations and distribution, to at least partially supplant the President and the Executive Office. The machinery established by CBICA does require almost simultaneous decisions on resource allocation and stabilization — and a specific approval of the size of the deficit (or surplus). The institutions also permit some flexibility in both program and fiscal policy decisions

17. It is at least interesting that in the second edition of *Public Finance in Theory and Practice*, Richard A. Musgrave and Peggy B. Musgrave, (New York: McGraw Hill, 1976) there is a new chapter on "The Theory of Optimal Distribution" that attempts to go beyond the vagueness of Wicksellian concepts of "proper" and "just" into the morass of Pareto-optimal income distribution based on interdependent utility functions.

as economic conditions change between January and September. In this sense CBICA appears to fit the neo-classical paradigm.

Until CBICA the Congress was presumably to reflect preferences for social goods, income distribution and stabilization, but the Executive had the responsibility for consolidating the "branches." Now Congress has a greater role in consolidation. However, the major issue in neo-classical fiscal theory is preference revelation and CBICA has little effect on this.

Incrementalism

Incrementalist fiscal theory, as defined here, is associated with the descriptive approach to budget-making dominated some years ago by Charles E. Lindblom and most recently by Aaron Wildavsky.[18] There are some rather sharp differences between the approach to government budgeting taken by these two scholars. For Lindblom consensus and agreement is to be maximized, and in the long run, efficiency in terms of survival. Wildavsky emphasizes political over economic values.

For Lindblom, conflicts are resolved by partisan mutual adjustment. Not all marginal values are examined at any one time. The strategy of decision consists of a selection process – of choices among the values to be costed out. In the real world means and ends are seldom specified or indeed separated. As the decision process proceeds on the basis of disjointed incrementalism, the policy maker is engaged in reconstructive leadership. He does not take preferences as given and attempt to interpret them; he is engaged in a dynamic process of interplay between his own values

18. The most relevant contributions by Lindblom are "Decision-Making in Taxation and Expenditures," in *Public Finances: Needs, Sources and Utilization* (Princeton: National Bureau of Economic Research, Princeton University Press, 1961), pp. 296–336; *The Policy-Making Process* (Englewood Cliffs: Prentice-Hill, 1968). Aaron Wildavsky, *Budgeting* (Boston: Little, Brown, 1975); *The Politics of the Budgetary Process*, 2nd ed., (Boston: Little, Brown, 1974); "Toward a Radical Incrementalism; A Proposal to Aid Congress in Reform of the Budgetary Process," in *Congress: The First Branch of Government* (Washington: American Enterprise Institute for Public Policy Research, 1965).
19. The Lindblomian paradigm has found greater support among students of political science and public administration than among economists. However, a recent effort to place it within the context of an economist's approach to budget-making is contained in Peter O. Steiner, "Public Expenditure Budgeting," in *The Economics of Public Finance* (Washington: The Brookings Institution, 1974), esp. pp. 257–282 where the author examines the "public interest" aspects of the original Dahl and Lindblom constructs.

and objectives and those of constituencies to whom he may be responsible.[19]

This view of budget-making has always had considerable appeal for practitioners; it appears to describe what, in fact, they do day by day. It would appear that a Lindblomian approach to budget-making is quite harmonious with the new Congressional fiscal institutions. The interplay among the House and Senate Budget Committees will not reduce the possibilities for reconstructive leadership, but should enhance them. The additional information flows from House and Senate budget committee staff and from the CBO, and, in particular, the analysis of budgetary trade-offs should enlighten and strengthen the budgetary process.

However, CBICA is not consonant with the view of the budgetary process advanced by the other major contemporary incrementalist – Wildavsky. In his analysis of the budgetary process political values are always more important than economic values. Annual budgeting should be replaced by continuous incremental budgeting; the costing out of alternatives, one of the major objectives of program budgeting, is treated with scorn. Attempts to introduce greater economic rationality into budget-making are doomed to fail. This appears to be Wildavsky's prediction about CBICA.[20]

Although the relationship between the Current Services Budget in November and the President's Budget in January is conceptually pure incrementalism, and thus could appeal to Wildavsky, he is most critical of efforts to build Congressional staff in competition with OMB. He feels that there will be a resulting information overload, diverting Congressmen from their basic responsibility of interpreting citizen preferences. Thus, CBICA procedures are essentially incrementalist, but the analytic work of CBO is anti-incrementalist.

Perhaps, more than others, incrementalists are entitled to second thoughts. Most recently Wildavsky has partially modified his position. In commenting on the continued tendency toward the dispersal of the powers of Congress, he now suggests that the only possible exception is the new budget reform:[21]

20. Testimony at hearings before the Subcommittee on Budgeting, Manegement, and Expenditures, Committee on Government Operations, U. S. Senate, *Improving Congressional Control of the Budget* 93rd Congress, 1st Session, Part 1, April 1973, pp. 388–397; 493–508.
21. Aaron Wildavsky, "The Past and Future Presidency" *Public Interest* Fall, 1975, p. 63.

> If successful, it would, by relating revenue to expenditure, enable Congress to maintain its power of the purse. But the prognosis is problematic . . . .
> If the new House and Senate budget committees attempt to act like cabinets on the British mold, which enforce their preferences on the legislature, they will fail . . . .
> If the budget committees permit too many deviations, or are over-ruled too often, it will become clear that expenditures are out of control. Power will pass to the Executive. Impoundment *de facto* will become impoundment *de jure.*

Incrementalists are quite clearly no more adept at forecasting fiscal outcomes than neo-classical economists. But Wildavsky has certainly pointed to the fundamental dilemma: the new budget committees must be strong enough to "control" but not so strong as to upset existing Congressional committee prerogatives. This point will be re-examined in the prognosis section of this paper.

Neo-Marxism

There is an emerging body of fiscal theory that attempts to fill a major gap in conventional Marxism — the theory of the state. In some of its dimensions this literature is germane to the problem at hand — an appraisal of the tax-expenditure role of governments.

There appear to be three strands to this literature.[22] The first has been called "instrumentalist" — an examination of the ways by which specific capitalist interests manipulate state policy, including the fisc, to accomplish their objectives. Ralph Miliband's writings would fall in this category.[23] The approach is often polemic, but does point to some interesting case studies that would provide insights into the relationships between the public and the private sectors. The instances of Penn-Central and Lockheed suggest that this would be a fertile field for investigation. However, the instrumentalist approach does not attempt to examine fiscal institutions or decision processes. As for CBICA, an instrumentalist could argue that these fiscal institutions will make more difficult the manipulation of the state by established interests.

A second strand has been called Hegelian-Marxist, emphasizing ideology, consciousness and alienation. Marcuse's writings would fall

22. See David A. Gold, Clarence Y. H. Le, Erik Olin Wright, "Recent Developments in Marxist Theories of the Capitalist State," *Monthly Review,* October 1975, pp. 29–43; November, pp. 36–51.
23. *The State in Capitalist Society* (London: Weidenfeld & Nicolson, 1969).

in this area. Again, this approach is not especially relevant to the behavior of fiscal institutions; the concern is directed very broadly toward the relationships of man to a capitalist society.

The third approach has been labeled "structuralist". James O'Connor's analysis is most relevant here.[24] The fiscal crisis is the continued tendency of governmental expenditure to outstrip governmental revenue. This occurs because the state, in advanced industrial society, must perform two contradictory functions: accumulation and legitimation. The former is the continued provision of social overhead capital to supplement and support private capital accumulation. The latter is the necessity for maintaining social peace and harmony, such as outlays for police and welfare. Expenditures on social overhead are indirectly productive of surplus value, but social expenses are not. Thus, in O'Connor's view, there is a continued and heightened political conflict fought in terms of the state budget; this conflict will intensify and not dimish.

It may be surmised that a neo-Marxist "structuralist" approach, which is directed toward an analysis of the contradictions and constraints that the market sector imposes on the public sector, would regard any effort to fashion new fiscal structures without changing the basic distribution of economic power — including CBICA — as fruitless. This kind of fatalism about public-private sector relationships is not, of course, confined to neo-Marxists. Schumpeter, in *Capitalism, Socialism and Democracy* had strikingly similarly views, and Galbraith is in some ways his contemporary counterpart.[25]

Public Choice

The fourth paradigm, and the one that is perhaps most relevant to an appraisal of CBICA, is public choice theory. This varied and massive literature is beginning to embrace topics far beyond the scope of the present inquiry in such areas as voting solutions, conflict resolution, and property rights. The portions of public choice theory that are most relevant here are the attention to the

24. *The Fiscal Crisis of the State* (New York: St. Martins, 1973) and the journal *Kapitalistate.*
25. New York: Harper & Row, 1950; John Kenneth Galbraith, testimony, Subcommittee on *Budgeting, Management, and Expenditure, op. cit.*, pp. 366–388.

role of fiscal institutions and the theory of bureaucracy.[26]

The basic assumption of public choice theory is that governments are collectivities of utility maximizers — elected officials, bureaucrats, judges, bureaus and agencies and clientele groups.[27] There is little room here for the public interest approach that characterizes the writings of such economists as Gerhard Colm or such political scientists as Paul Appleby.[28] As utility maximizers, decision makers pursue their gains from trade. The propensity to truck, barter and exchange is the operational mechanism.

The fiscal theory portions of public choice are directed to such matters as the conditions under which collective choice will yield an optimum, as compared with individualistic, market solutions, and thus considerable attention is directed to information costs, agreement costs and transactions costs. Attention is also directed to the effects of alternative fiscal institutions — on the private sector and on persons and groups in the public sector. Public choice is also concerned with differences that result when rules are applied to constitutional, statutory and bureaucratic levels. Wagner has quoted with approval Wicksell's statement that ". . . the primary task for fiscal theory was not to specify the conditions for fiscal efficiency, but was to specify the institutional framework within which efficient budgets will be chosen."[29] Buchanan's contention that the study of fiscal institutions has been seriously neglected is evidently the case.

Thus, public choice theory, unlike the neo-classical approach, is very much concerned with the kind of institutional change represented by CBICA. However, public choice theorists would appear to be caught in a dilemma in the application of their paradigm to CBICA. Their policy prescriptions in public finance invariably favor the decentralization of authority, a preference for reducing the size of the public sector, or at least reducing its rate of

26. Representative and relevant literature includes James M. Buchanan and Gordon Tullock, *The Calculus of Consent* (Ann Arbor: University of Michigan Press, 1962); James M. Buchanan, *The Demand and Supply of Public Goods* (Chicago: Rand McNally, 1968); Richard E. Wagner, *The Public Economy* (Chicago: Markham, 1973); Gordon Tullock, *The Politics of Bureaucracy* (Washington: Public Affairs Press, 1965); William Niskanen, *Bureaucracy and Representative Government* (Chicago: Aldine, 1971).
27. James M. Buchanan, "Public Finance and Public Choice," *National Tax Journal*, December 1975, p. 389.
28. See Burkhead and Miner, *op. cit.*, pp. 156–163.
29. Richard Wagner, *The Fiscal Organization of American Federalism*, (Chicago: Markham, 1971), p. 7.

growth, and, in particular a preference for reducing the size of the national government. Thus, the fiscal institutions established by CBICA could be approved on the ground that they may reduce the size of the national government. But they could be disapproved on the ground that they contribute to a centralization of fiscal authority – this time in the hands of the Congress rather than in the hands of the Executive. There are now two competing centralizing forces each with competing objective functions to maximize.

At this point it might be useful to reverse the methodology and ask, not what does the paradigm suggest about the outcomes of changes in fiscal institutions, but rather, how will the changes in fiscal institutions strengthen or weaken the several models that are available? Alternatively, how will the change in fiscal institutions contribute to the viability of the available theories?

This approach would commit this paper to a methodological inquiry that could be the subject of a second essay. What contributes to operationalism? What gaps are filled as information load is increased? What are the opportunity costs of information? How does a change in fiscal institutions affect the conventional questions posed by fiscal theory: preference revelation, agreement costs, the analytic studies of tradeoffs, the role of interest groups in preference intensity? It is always possible that a change in fiscal institutions could fulfill the requirements of a specific fiscal theory and still end up as operational failure.

Perhaps we should not ask too much of fiscal theory, but it must be concluded that none of the existing fiscal paradigms is completely satisfactory as an analytic tool-box for predicting the outcome of CBICA. Thus, it is necessary to undertake a limited case study of the 1975 experience and to draw whatever inferences are possible from this experience. This becomes heavily descriptive; the analytic content is meager.

6.3. Prospect

The overwhelming House and Senate majorities that voted for CBICA suggest the validity of an important point once made by Lindblom – in complex decision processes it is not necessary to assure agreement on ends; it is only necessary to assure agreement on means. Certainly the supporters of CBICA had differing and conflicting objective functions. There was agreement on only one point, that reform of Congressional budget-making was necessary.

What is Success?

The record of hearings, floor debate and voting suggest that there were three influences at work. The first of these may be called "constitutionalism" — the desire on the part of the Congress to restore its "rightful" place in the budgetary process. In the words of Senator Sam Ervin, "The time has come to restore the constitutional balance of power over the budget."[30] Or, in the words of the Senate Report:

> At stake, therefore, in the attempt to improve the spending process, is the restoration to Congress of its essential role in American Government.[31]

This, of course, was the reaction to the Imperial Presidency, shared by liberals and conservatives alike.

The second influence was conservatism — the hope that new fiscal institutions would reduce federal spending. This viewpoint was well expressed by Senator Talmadge, "By placing ceilings on Federal expenditures, this bill may lead to much-needed cutbacks in extravagant and unnecessary programs."[32]

The third influence was liberalism, and although this is more difficult to document with specific statements, it may certainly be inferred from behavior patterns. The liberals hoped that the House and Senate Budget Committees would counteract the traditional conservatism of House Ways and Means, Senate Finance, and the House and Senate Appropriations Committees. In addition, the liberal members of the Congress anticipated that the impoundments that had reduced or eliminated social programs would be greatly curtailed.

Clearly, CBICA meant a number of things to a number of people. The strong consensus vote is reminiscent of the overwhelming majority that adopted the Employment Act of 1946. These multiple and conflicting objectives make appraisal of the FY 1976

---

30. *Congressional Record*, March 19, 1974, p. S3832.
31. Senate Committee on Government Operations, *Federal Act to Control Expenditures and Establish National Priorities*, Report 93–579, 93rd Congress.
32. *Congressional Record*, March 20, 1974, p. 3998.

experiences and prognosis for the future even more treacherous. How is it possible to appraise success ". . . beyond our most optimistic expectations," as Senator Muskie stated last December, when there are conflicting ιriteria for judging success?

Prognosis must rest on the one-year experience in 1975. The concurrent resolutions were adopted. The Budget Committees and the CBO were staffed and began to issue reports. The Current Services Budget was produced as scheduled. The Joint Economic Committee responded. The ceiling provisions were significant in limiting specific appropriations measures, from the DOD to school lunch appropriations.

So, this must all be judged "success." However, before excessive optimism prevails it should be noted that there were several idiosyncratic factors at work in actions on the FY 1976 budget. This was a trial run and the time-table was not strictly binding. Congressmen perceived the Budget Committees to be prestigious and this enhanced the power positions of those committees. The two chairmen — Congressman Adams and Senator Muskie — took their responsibilities seriously. Congressmen apparently felt that their institutional prestige was threatened and wished to make the new law operative. The size and quality of Budget Committee staffs and of the CBO staff facilitated an unusually rapid and high-quality information flow.

There were also idiosyncratic Executive Office factors at work. The non-elected President did not enjoy high prestige. Apparently responding to conservative influences on the political right, the President continued to urge a fiscal policy of great restraint, a policy that was generally rejected by a neo-Keynesian Congressional majority. The President also continued to utilize impoundment.[33]

Further, the departments and agencies appear to be comfortable with the new fiscal institutions. Forward projections are harmonious with the kind of budget-making that departments and agencies practice. The new Budget Committees and CBO provide additional channels for departments and agencies to influence Congressional action. OMB can more easily be circumvented.

Finally, some outside influences were at work. In a year of serious recession the large deficit appeared to frighten few Congressmen,

33. For a review of impoundment since the enactment of CBICA, see Allen Schick, *The Impoundment Control Act of 1974: Legislative History and Implementation* (Washington, D. C.: CRS, 1976).

which must mean that it frightened few of their constituents. The business community was certainly not unanimous in opposing fiscal stimulus. And if a head-count were to be taken in the academic world, in the unlikely event that such a count would be significant, it would be possible to find more economists who favored more fiscal stimulus than those in opposition, where fiscal stimulus is measured solely in the simplistic terms of the size of the federal deficit.

In one respect the FY 1976 experience was as bad or worse than in previous years. As noted earlier, appropriation bills have been signed later and later. The trial run did not improve matters. As of January 1, 1976 action had not yet been completed on four appropriation measures. This is the worst record since FY 1971, but this may not be a significant criterion for judging success.[34]

"The Budget is Out of Control"

There are at least four connotations in which this phrase is used. "Out of Control" means that the size of the national government sector is too large in relation to some magnitude, such as national income or GNP. Second, the phrase may refer to the increase in "backdoor spending." Third, there is a technical meaning to "relative controllability" in terms of what the Administration or the Congress can do in any one year without altering existing legislation. Fourth, the phrase sometimes means that the Congress is "out of control" and engaged in wasteful and profligate spending.[35]

It is difficult to untangle these inter-related concepts but some brief comments on each are appropriate.

Anyone who has had the misfortune to struggle with ratios of government activity to the total of national economic activity is well aware of the thicket in which (s)he is working. There is simply no agreement among students of public finance as to the appropriate numerator, the appropriate denominator, and hence the appropriate ratio. Should transfer payments be included in the

34. As far as can be ascertained the Congress has not been able to complete action on all appropriation bills before the beginning of the fiscal year since FY 1949.
35. The 1976 *Priorities* volume suggests another definition in terms of the flexibility of fiscal policy. See Blechman, et. al., pp. 190–230. An additional definition in terms of uncontrollable increments could also be specified.

numerator, or only goods and service transactions? Are the operations of public enterprise, such as the Postal Service, to be treated at gross or net? Should the financial sector – loans, loan guarantees, interest on loans and repayments – be counted in or out? The denominator difficulties are similar – should it be GNP, NNP, national income, personal income or full employment GNP? Is federal sector expenditure as a percentage of GNP the best measure?

Those who have labored in these peat bogs usually emerge with a series of measures – Variant I, Variant II, Variant III. This, at least is a relatively safe haven for the frustrated statistician.[36]

A limited number of observations may be in order. As noted above, the ratio of federal expenditures to GNP, one of the most commonly employed numbers, increased from 19.8 percent in FY 1961 to 23.5 percent fifteen years later in FY 1976. This is 3.7 percentage points and an 18.7 percent increase for an annual average of 1.2 percent. Those who are alarmed about the growth in the national government might well project this ratio, compound it annually, and become frightened. However, federal sector expenditures as a percentage of GNP, according to the 1977 *Budget* were 20.0 in FY 1967 and are estimated at 22.0 for FY 1977. This is an average annual increase of one percent.

Federal budget outlays in relation to full employment GNP increased from 17.3 percent in FY 1960 to an estimated 19.6 percent in FY 1976. This is 2.3 percentage points or 13.3 percent but would probably be reduced if appropriate allowance could be made for differentials in federal sector prices as compared with private sector prices for goods and services.[37]

As for near-term projections of current services, the Congressional Budget Office has defined Path A, with an average annual increase in the GNP deflator of 6.7 percent, and a growth rate in real GNP of 6 percent between 1975 and 1981. This yields an estimate of the costs of continuing existing federal programs that produces a budget surplus of $92 billion in 1981. Path B, with an average deflator of 5.8 percent and a real GNP growth rate of 5 percent does not eliminate the federal budget deficit until after 1981 –

36. Senator Goldwater has estimated that on July 4, 1988 total government spending will be 50.8 percent of national income. *Congressional Record*, Senate, August 13, 1974, p. 106.
37. Blechman, *et. al.*, pp. 4–7.

again, with no new programs. But, if budget policy is predicated on the full employment surplus, Path A yields a budget margin of $116 billion in 1981 and Path B yields a $68 billion margin.[38] If one believes in the full employment surplus as the appropriate budget target, a belief that has been shared intermittently by Presidents Kennedy, Johnson, Nixon and Ford, we will need tax reduction or new spending programs by FY 1981 to avoid serious fiscal restraint.

The second assertion — that the budget is out of control because "backdoor spending" has increased and hence in any one budget year the uncontrollables are a very large portion of budget outlays, is, indeed, the case. Prior-year commitments, entitlements and contract authority have substantially increased in recent years, but precise numerical comparisons are not available.[39] This is a good part of what CBICA is all about and if the new institutions work, the future year implications of this year's authorizations will be much better understood. This theme runs through almost every report issued by the Congressional Budget Office. But experience is necessary before it can be determined that the appropriations committees will, in fact, begin to control "backdoor spending."

The third concept of "uncontrollable" is the one used in the U. S. Budget: outlays are defined as relatively uncontrollable in any one year when the President's decisions in that year can neither increase nor decrease them without a change in substantive law.[40] On this definition, "relatively uncontrollable" has increased from 59 percent of budget outlays in FY 1967 to 73 percent in FY 1976, is estimated at 77 percent in FY 1977 and projected to decline to 58 percent in FY 1981, if no new programs are enacted.[41]

The fourth concept of "out of control" — the charge of Congressional over-spending — is particularly difficult to analyze. No consistent time series appears to be available to permit a comparison of what the President proposes and what the Congress disposes. Available data are difficult to interpret as between budget

38. Congressional Budget Office, *Five Year Budget Projections, Fiscal Years 1977–1981* (Washington: January 1976). The Administration's projections are in *The Budget of the United States Government, Fiscal Year 1977*, (Washington, 1976), pp. 24–37.
39. Contract authority and authority to spend from public debt receipts were 12.4 percent of total budget outlays in FY 1974, 21.9 percent in FY 1975 and are estimated in the 1977 *Budget* at 12.5 percent for FY 1976 and 9.5 percent for FY 1977. *The Budget* does not publish time series data on permanent appropriations and entitlements.
40. *The Budget of the United States Government*, Fiscal Year 1977, (Washington, 1976), p. 6.
41. *Ibid.*, pp. 34, 355.

authority and budget outlay, as between regular and supplemental appropriations. Furthermore, impoundments ought somehow to enter into a comparison of Executive actions with Congressional actions.

On the basis of scorekeeping reports, in recent years the Congress has reduced regular appropriations below those submitted by the Executive. For the years 1969–73 such reductions appear to have amounted to $30.8 billion.[42] However, in these same years the Congress added $30.4 billion by way of "backdoor spending." Thus, Congress did not increase total spending over Administration requests; the type of spending authority was changed.

It is not possible to make accurate comparisons of Executive budget policy with Congressional budget policy. There are too many intervening variables — supplementals, impoundments, vetoes that may be sustained or over ridden. Moreover, new authorizations by the Congress in one fiscal year may become incorporated in the President's budget in the following fiscal year — a case of joint responsibility. However, there was an attempt to make such comparisons for FY 69–73 and the numbers that emerge are at least interesting. In these years a comparison of Executive budget estimates submitted with realized budget deficits shows the latter to be $44.6 billion greater. Congressional actions would thus appear to have increased the budget deficit by an average of $8.9 billion a year in budget outlays.[43] If outlays alone are examined, the average increase by Congress in this period was even smaller — $3.5 billion. These numbers do not make a strong case for Congressional irresponsibility in the period preceding the enactment of CBICA.

Under the dry-run FY 1976 procedures the second concurrent resolution increased budget authority by $14.3 billion more than the President's requests and increased budget outlays by $8.0 billion more than requested.[44] It is not possible to compare the proposed Presidential deficit with the resulting (estimated) Congressionally-approved deficit because of the difficulty of interpreting the President's revenue proposals after the veto, then the approval of the tax extension bill in December 1975.

42. U. S. Congress. Special Joint Committee on Budget Control, *Recommendations for Improving Congressional Control Over Budgetary Outlay and Receipt Totals*, Washington, D. C. (February 7, 1975).
43. House Report 93–113, 1973, p. 16.
44. Congressional Budget Office, Staff Working Paper for 1976 *Congressional Budget Scorekeeping* (Washington, 1975) p. 2.

The scorecard on controllability thus stands as follows:

First, those who are alarmed by an average annual increase in the ratio of federal expenditures to GNP of 1.2 percent since 1961 will conclude that the budget is out of control. Those who look at federal expenditures in relation to the full employment budget are not likely to be concerned at an annual average increase of one-half percent.

Second, those who associate "out of control" with the "backdoor spending" concept employed in the Budget can certainly be alarmed about recent developments, but should take heart at the projected decline in this ratio for FY 1981.

Third, those who center attention on the "relatively uncontrollable" concept employed in the Budget can certainly be alarmed about recent developments, but should take heart at the projected decline in this ratio for FY 1981.

Fourth, those who argue that the budget is out of control because of Congressional profligacy have a rather weak case that must rest on numbers averaging $3 billion a year. But if the trial run is any test, CBICA comes off badly since the Congress increased budget outlays far more than recent average experience. However, this was a year in which fiscal stimulus was widely approved.

Winners and Losers

Some outstanding scholars in political science have provided, down the years, substantial insights into Congressional decision-making in fiscal affairs by their careful case studies of the relationships among subcommittees, committees, House and Senate leadership and resulting impacts on legislative outcomes. This research dates at least as far back as the Macmahon articles in the 1940s.[45] In recent years this tradition has been continued by Fenno.[46] It can only be hoped that a Fenno will, five or six years from now, analyze in depth the fiscal institutions established by CBICA in 1974. At this point, in the absence of such in-depth analysis over time, prognosis

---

45. Arthur W. Macmahon, "Congressional Oversight of Administration: The Power of the Purse," *Political Science Quarterly*, June 1943, pp. 161–190; September, 1943, pp. 380–414.
46. Ricahrd F. Fenno, *The Power of the Purse: Appropriations Politics in Congress* (Boston: Little, Brown, 1966) and *Congressmen in Committees* (Boston: Little, Brown, 1973).

of the outcome of CBICA is necessary but very nearly idle speculation.

On the surface CBICA is " . . . a masterpiece of changing procedures in an important way without challenging existing power centers."[47] But in fact, there must be some shifts in Congressional power centers and shifts in decision authority between the Congress and the Executive if CBICA is not to be meaningless. It is not clear that this is a matter of game theory or gamesmanship. It is more likely to be tic-tac-toe, where, with two equally intelligent players, the cat wins. Moreover, an examination of one change in the power structure without a study of the totality of the power structure does not permit a perception of power-diffusion or power-concentration consequences.[48]

The following speculations appear to be appropriate.

In Congress:

1. The Joint Economic Committee is relatively undisturbed and has a small piece of the action.
2. The Joint Committee on Internal Revenue Taxation, and House Ways and Means will lose some authority over both revenue and spending legislation. Senate Finance is more likely to gain initiative but lose authority. The House and Senate Budget Committees will inevitably become increasingly involved with revenue measures.
3. The stage has been set for a struggle over power, prestige and possession between the Budget Committees and the subcommittees of the House and Senate Appropriations Committees. This will be crucial, as Wildavsky has pointed out.
4. The General Accounting Office and the Comptroller General, who have gradually increased their influence on the budgetary process, will continue to expand their power base.

On the Executive side, the outlook is even more murky:

1. The Executive Office, including the Presidency, may suffer a loss

47. Pfiffner, *op. cit.*, p. 12.
48. Warren J. Samuels, "On Some Fundamental Issues in Political Economy: An Exchange of Correspondence," (with James M. Buchanan), *Journal of Economic Issues*, March 1975, p. 31.

in budgetary authority largely due to the curtailment of impoundment power.

2. Within the Executive Office, OMB may be somewhat strengthened, since it, too, will be possessed of additional information that flows to the Congress from the departments and agencies.

3. The Council of Economic Advisers will face a more competitive environment, with the competition coming from the staffs of the Budget Committees and the CBO.

4. It is simply not possible to anticipate what will happen to departments and agencies and their budget staffs, *vis a vis* OMB or *vis a vis* Congressional committees.

On other matters, the representatives of interest groups, usually called lobbyists, must expand their range of activities to include the Budget Committees, their staffs, and the CBO.

CBO faces many problems. It must maintain good working relations with standing committees and with the House and Senate Budget Committees and their staffs. Scorekeeping on the fiscal implications of thousands of bills introduced in the Congress each year is a monumental task. Projections, even when hedged by the most careful assumptions, are always hazardous and a few bad projections may discredit CBO. It has already come under attack for this and other reasons.[49] As for CBICA procedures, the timetable is very tight and threatens the summer vacations of members of the appropriations committees.

Perhaps it is all a mistake, that will soon go the way of previous efforts at Congressional budgetary reform. It may be that Congress should not build large staffs to generate a very large information flow and that Congress should not attempt to compete with the bureaucracy.[50] Chances for "success," judged on the basis of any criterion that could be suggested, cannot be put at more than fifty-fifty.

The final observation is that, if the fiscal institutions established by CBICA do succeed in rationalizing the role of Congress in budget-making, such institutions will fit .very well into the kind of

49. See the comments of Congressman Latta on October 8, 1975, *Congressional Record* 121:151, pp. H9782–9784. See also Joel Havemann, "Budget Report/CBO Proceeds With Work While Taking Heat on Staff Size," *National Journal* 7:46 (November 15, 1976), pp. 1575–1577.
50. On the other hand, Congressmen will certainly become better informed on the macro aspects of budgeting and on future year implications of current actions.

economic planning that is proposed under Humphrey-Javits (S1795). This would be a startling outcome for those conservatives in the Congress who approved budget reform in the hope that it would reduce the role of the federal government in the national economy.

The Congress may well have fashioned the machinery for Congressional-Administration planning, in an admixture of pragmatism and pluralism, preserving the most unusual representative democracy extant. CBICA may be a major step toward National Economic Planning.

COMMENTS

C. Lowell Harriss

The authors in this excellent paper discuss many aspects of the background, features, and prospects of this major undertaking. For reasons they suggest, it may become in fact an outstanding innovation. Or it may accomplish rather little. Because its many sponsors were hoping for a variety of results, not all of which would be consistent with each other, the evaluations of what does develop will almost inevitably differ markedly.

1. Importance

The subject, "controlling" the growth of Federal spending, has greater significance for human life than the authors may seem to imply. Politicians and civil servants are disposing of the "other fellow's" money on a huge scale – per capita Federal spending of over $1,850 a year and taxes around $1,550. Do not elementary principles of responsible conduct call for the most exacting standards in making decisions? To quote with apparent approval a statement to the effect that the share of total output consumed by the Federal government has changed "relatively little" may understate the importance of what is at issue.[1] Later the authors do discuss various concepts of "out of control." Their undertaking does not require explicit concern with the meaning of "too large." But can we not all agree that the amounts *are* very great indeed? Such size has enormous bearing on the importance of making better rather than poorer decisions.

Not only are the dollar amounts of possible "waste" large enough to be of great significance, but the budget reforms do not explicitly embody changes for better operating performance. Perhaps, however, new pressures will develop out of changes in budget procedures to make dollars serve more efficiently.

Another dimension has even more significance for "the good society." Again, one hopes that the reform procedures will help even though framers did not provide explicitly for assistance in confronting the issue: An allocation (1) between the private and the political sectors and (2) among the many governmental programs. Some of the ends sought in collective action, and the means used, do mean much to all of us. Running this huge portion of "our" affairs as well as possible should rank high on the agenda of things to be done. The efforts of Congress to do a better job are to be welcomed. They do not, however, embrace all of the task. What do people *really* want? The new procedures may somehow contribute a little.

Perhaps the taxpayer will gain. But the reform by no means assures that spending will be (much) (1) smaller or (2) better than otherwise.

2. The Reform Structure and Timetable

The summary of the background, the new organization, and the new timetable provides a helpful framework. Yet space limits precluded a report of why earlier efforts failed. The authors call attention to the overwhelming support in both houses for the final version. The reasons for such support differed so much that

1. They are by no means the first to say that Federal spending has not grown "much" in relation to a rising GNP. We also hear at times that government spending in this country is not so large as in some others. Both assertions can be correct but nonetheless mislead. Issues of (1) political as against (2) market-philanthropic-voluntary use of resources remain for serious attention. How well do politicians and bureaucrats and the military decide on employing our income? What other countries do is not necessarily best for them; even if it were, what the British or Italians or Japanese do would not for that reason necessarily be best for the U. S. Moreover, the rise of spending involves not only dollars of outlay but also the myriads of controls which can attach to the spending of Federal dollars – with leverage effects of no small size on individuals, universities, businesses, and state-local governments which must alter their behavior. Nor do the dollar plus the "control" effects include all those flowing from rising Federal outlays. Taxes and borrowing have their own direct and indirect results – excess burdens, externalities, spill-overs, and neighborhood and third-party influences on life.

consensus may not appear in actual implementation.

The actual accomplishments must reflect decisions on matters which will involve conflicts that mean a lot to Congressmen, the bureaucracy, various "clientele" groups. The allocations among programs will go to the heart of conflicts of utmost importance to the participants and their supporters. What kind of behavior, what gamesmanship and new techniques, may be developed to succeed over rivals in the new procedures? Will the new committees get a solid base of power? Only time will tell how the redistribution of power will develop and its effects. One casualty may be the reform itself.

The new timetable attempts to force what would seem to be a more rational procedure. Change in the sequence of stages, though of some potential for more logical action, is less striking than the timing. The new schedule is rigorous and tight. Key decisions must be made months earlier than has been the case. Will the new timing be possible?

What had developed was not the result of lazy procrastination or mere cussedness or blind naivete, of meaningless struggles for power. The long months taken in making decisions to authorize programs and to decide on appropriations often reflected difficulties which inhere in complexities of many types. The Federal government's many programs are not all simple enough to permit of early decisions. Changing the schedule does not in itself alter the underlying realities of a government of hundreds of programs which have importance for constituents of members of Congress. And when pressure to act earlier becomes powerful, the results will not necessarily be better. In seeking to improve the decisions on the aggregates, the new budget process may lead to less well considered actions on some of the constituent items.

The rigidity of the new schedule may hamper short-run responses for stabilization purposes. Although to date the record of fiscal policy action to offset undesired changes in the private economy may not get loud plaudits for successes, hope may remain. The new rules do tend to freeze Congress, more or less, into patterns for the period ahead. They will be difficult to modify if the outlook of the economy changes. Another obstacle to good timing of which we have dreamed seems to have been erected.

3. Fiscal Theory and Decision Structures

The section that examines briefly four theories of collective choice, is without counterpart in other writings I have seen on budget reform. Do these theories help in understanding the background for change of process and the possible results? The new procedures may enable Congress to combine more effectively the three "branches" of decision-making — allocation, distribution, and stabilization; the three aspects exist and involve actions which must be done — the question is by what means, with what explicit attention to the distinguishable elements, and how well. Perhaps if the Congressional movers in the new process are alerted to this tripartite aspect, they will achieve better results. But the allocation and distributive aspects involve complex issues of real rivalry and conflict. The Legislative Branch now has a better opportunity to "look at things whole." Perhaps the new staff work will make a helpful contribution.

The authors in looking for guidance seem inclined to draw upon the "Public Choice" approach with special reference to the interests and incentives of the participants. How will the people who have new power be moved in trying to use it? What will be their incentives? Another instrument for centralization — more unification of budget authority in the Legislative Branch, as an addition to that in the Executive Branch — has been created. If the new system operates according to the apparent intent, will not the hundreds of individual elements of this massive government be subordinated to the power of persons making decisions about the big aggregates?

4. A New Staff (Bureaucracy) and More Studies[2]

The new system with staffs of perhaps 350 creates new centers of influence and power. Another bureaucracy! "Knowledge is power," we have been told. More studies and analyses are to become available. Computer print-outs will flow in larger quantity. The authors discuss some of the implications. Explicit efforts to present options are welcome.

During the post-World War II discussions of Congressional

---

2. The new group will work and live in the Washington area. The attitudes and impressions and biases of the nation's capital will thus get another re-enforcement.

inadequacy, emphasis was laid on the need for more staff aid. A quarter of a century witnessed no small multiplication of Congressional staffs before the new budget law. Now there are more. How good will their work be? Who will utilize the material? How can Congressmen select the best analyses? Which members of the Committees will be able to make effective use of more studies?

An academician will applaud scholarship for aiding those in charge of the "public business." But not everything will be of the best quality and deserving of respect as a guide to action. The impressiveness of computer runs, and of results expressed with great precision, may exceed their true merit.

Despite the efforts which will be made by the leaders of the Congressional groups, and despite what may be scrutiny from the Executive Branch, outside monitoring of research work will probably be desirable. Some non-official staffs of ample competence ought to be available on a continuing basis to review the technical work. The public and members of Congress can benefit from help from persons really qualified to scrutinize models and assumptions, the quality of figures and other inputs, and the interpretations of findings. A governmental staff study getting the designation "official" may not in fact be of highest quality, exhaustive, and deserving of respect as truly authoritative for guiding action. Professional staffs may not themselves be aware of all weaknesses. Or recognizing limitations of their work, they may be unwilling to protest when someone else (e.g., a member of Congress or a top official in the Executive Branch) misuses a study perhaps for purposes more expedient politically than statesmanlike.

5. Lengthening the Perspective in Decision-Making

The new rules require that more attention be given to the longer-run implications of spending proposals. Figures estimating expenditures for five years can certainly help to provide perspective better than what has been common. True, there are no personal penalties for projecting poorly; civil servants and Congressmen are not committing their own funds as does a business firm in making decisions for the future. Yet serious efforts to bring the future into consideration before actions are taken ought to improve the quality of governmental policy in the sense that decisions come closer to those voters would "really" prefer.

6. Judging Success

Because the goals of the supporters differed greatly, the authors show that judging success or failure must itself involve conflicts. Caution is called for, and what some observers would term success others would view differently. The authors warn us to be on the alert. The future may be quite different from the hopes of any one group of supporters – and not all of them can be satisfied.

The discussion of probable redistribution of influences within government suggests points to observe. Personalities, of course, will play a large role. Incidentally, the list of possible "winners" does not include the taxpayer or the ordinary person – or those of us who would welcome a reduction in the extent of political-bureaucratic control. For the near term, some slowing of the growth of spending seems probable. The total job to be done is vastly extensive – in getting the "right" totals of spending and taxing, in financing deficits and surpluses "correctly," in the allocation of spending as wisely as possible among hundreds of programs, in raising taxes with the minimum of adverse effects, and so on. And there will inevitably remain basic issues of the size and nature of the role of politics and bureaucracy.

7. Economic Planning

The concluding paragraph suggests that success of the reform procedures would assist in implementing economic planning as now being advocated. The authors do not spell out their thoughts. But more centralization of decisions on what is a substantial fraction of the country's affairs – Federal spending, taxing, and borrowing – would perhaps do part of what supporters of planning envisage.

Another observation: The efforts to reform the budget process, the "government's very own affairs," will illuminate some of the many difficulties, very great difficulties, of centralized, integrated "management" of a huge, ever-changing, and enormously diverse economy.

8. Concluding Comment

The authors alert us to the fact that the procedures are less than two years old and are only this year being tested fully. Only as time passes will the actual effects become reasonably clear. (One can never know what would have developed otherwise.) Even if the results do come close to meeting the high hopes of sponsors, the new *procedures* will not assure that the *substance* will approach something optimal. Congress must still decide on the totals. It must still allocate limited funds among competing programs. It must still decide on the structure of tax laws.

A better base of information should lead to better decisions. One role for academicians and others outside government will be assisting in the continuing improvement of evidence, facts, and analysis.

Warren J. Samuels

This is a paper by professionals who retain and develop their perspective in the face of considerable opportunity for dogmatic assertion and wishful thinking. It is sensible, straightforward, and nonpartisan in its historical perspective, summary of CBICA and its status, consideration of fiscal theories, and evaluation of that new shibboleth of the politics of "responsibility," that the "budget is out of control." Theirs is a perspective of staying close to the facts and of caution against premature jumping to conclusions. Accordingly, the paper may not be very satisfying to both strong partisans and those who want one-and-for-all-time solutions to problems.

The paper is directly concerned with the budgetary process in a representative democracy. The key question which it, along with much related literature, poses for me is: What do we have other than ideology to inform us as to how large or small the budget should be and/or of what it should consist? Moreover, is that a meaningful question? Idealist theories of the public interest and of public choice assert some *a priori* answer; realist theories assert that we have to look only to the legislative process itself. In both cases, what is there to work with other than ideology? A further question which arises in my mind is: What power positions are served by particular ideological assertions under given specific circumstances? I will return to the key question; as for the latter question, I raise it only to get on the record the point that ideological assertions *do* have coefficients of meaning reckoned in terms of the power positions which they serve, however ambiguous, uncertain, or problematical is that service.

One thing which we do not know very much about are the likely performance consequences of institutional innovation. Actually, I think that we know more than we consciously recognize. However, as economists we have been preoccupied with esoteria and presumptive evaluation rather than with detailed empirical investigations of what differences are made by new institutional adjustments. It is to his credit that much of Professor Burkhead's past work is an exception to the general rule. Perhaps in a decade or so we shall have better insight into the consequences of CBICA for the level and structure of spending and, possibly also, taxing.

Key to this insight will be an appreciation that the new institutional innovations (and their future adjustments) must be interpreted within the larger structure and process of political and economic power and that they form not a solution as such but a new arena within which fiscal policy is to be made. We will continue inevitably with the struggle for power, with fiscal politics. As for performance consequences, without fundamental changes in the structure of power no major changes therein are likely, *ceteris paribus* exogenous factors. But, then, perhaps the most we can ever hope for are small, and not large, favors. Apropos considerations of power, however, to which the present paper is unusually sensitive, I refer interested parties to Randall Bartlett's suggestive opus, *The Economic Foundations of Political Power* (Free Press, 1973; reviewed by me in *Journal of Economic Issues*, March 1976), especially if one is interested in an open-ended approach to the economics of information – for it is so-called "better" information which is said to be a main product of CBO and the entire new budgetary system.

Let me move to and treat all too cursorily a serious interpretive problem. One of the limits of traditional budgetary analysis is that it treats governmental fiscal accounts, whether or not in balance, as the measure of government activity. This is a gross misconception regardless of politico-ideological position: There are uses of government which are highly manifest through the level and/or structure of the budget but there are other uses of government which either do not at all show up in or are not adequately revealed in the budget accounts. We have made a start in this direction through the estimation of tax expenditures. But there are also rights, property and nonproperty, which are defined and assigned through government and an inevitable array of opportunities for private gain (and loss) similarly created and distributed by government. Some persons' interests are promoted by government action clearly reflected in the budget; others' are not. One type is called subsidies and/or the welfare state; the other is called the business system.

Somewhat related to this, in connection with the so-called Wicksellian notion of efficient budgets, let me say that there is a vast array of conceptually possible efficient budgets, each depending upon whose rights govern the substance of efficiency. Jockeying for position to govern the effective rights forming the so-called efficient budget is what fiscal politics is all about.

It seems to me that two of the most heuristically pregnant statements ever made concerning fiscal politics involve the nature of fiscal control as a handle with which to control the state and the social structure. Rudolf Goldschied wrote:

> The rising bourgeois classes wanted a poor State, a State depending for its revenue on their good graces, because these classes knew their own power to depend upon what the State did or did not have money for.
> ... The State became the instrument of the ruling classes by the fiscal organization which they imposed upon it. Capitalists have used the public household on the largest scale to enhance their profits and extend their power since capitalism has emerged triumphant in the form of financial capital.[1]

Joseph Schumpeter wrote:

> The kind and level of taxes are determined by the social structure, but once taxes exist they become a handle, as it were, which social powers can grip in order to change this structure.[2]

Consider, if you will, the term "fiscal responsibility." The "responsibility" part of it is quite ambiguous. Among other things, on the one hand, to be responsible means to have adequate power to effectuate assigned or expected duties; on the other, to be responsible means to be accountable, which is to say, to have limited power. A critical issue involves the definition of assigned or expected duties. Each notion of responsibility functions to promote

1. Rudolf Goldscheid, "A Sociological Approach to Problems of Public Finance," in R. A. Musgrave and A. T. Peacock, eds., *Classics In The Theory of Public Finance* (London: Macmillan, 1967), pp. 205–211.
2. Joseph A. Schumpeter, "The Crisis of the Tax State," *International Economic Papers*, 1954, p. 17.

a use or set of uses of government, and deals with substance while often seeming to relate only to financial decision-making procedure. Each notion of responsibility is a device with which to insinuate a theory of the control of government and is inherently neither for nor against government per se. Responsibility, then, is a function of point of view, or is largely so, certainly in the areas of controversy. A specific current example is governmental accrual accounting.[3] Without regard to the informational merits of and limits to such accounting, my point is that proponents seek to use it to direct fiscal "responsibility" in one direction rather than another. Responsibility may well depend upon whose prospective goose is likely to get cooked, except that both the cooking process and the culinary results are typically ambiguous. Compare the different connotations of responsibility attributed to CBICA and to the National Economic Planning bill, whether or not the former is a major step toward the latter.

As for the various theories of collective choice with regard to fiscal matters, let me make the following points: We need to differentiate carefully between the normative and positive elements or aspects of each. We then would be more knowledgeable as to what are the evaluative-prescriptive and the explanatory facets of each, and more able to discriminate between conservative and/or radical uses of theories *vis-a-vis* their heuristic descriptive and/or explanatory uses. We might also be able to see commonalities among the theories, points which are stated in different forms in different theories. Realist public interest theory and descriptive public choice and incrementalist theories have much in common. Furthermore, we need to conduct careful research into the various lines of reasoning which lead to the conclusions of over- versus under production of technical public goods, government goods generally, and government budgets. What we have now is a collection of lines of reasoning with little if any substantive insight into the criteria for comparing, not to say evaluating, them. We seem to elect one or the other largely upon ideological or circumstantial bases.

I am not saying that we lack scholarship in these areas. We have it,

---

3. Arthur Andersen & Co., *Sound Financial Reporting in the Public Sector: A Prerequisite to Fiscal Responsibility* (1975); Fiscal and Economic Policy Department, National Association of Manufacturers, *Government Operations/Expenditures Report*, "Accrual Accounting for Government?", February 3, 1976.

although we could use more. What I am getting at, rather, is the inevitability of our existential anguish over the size and substance of the government's budget. This is part of the larger problem, insoluble permanently, of the economic role of government. Other parts include the ambiguities of private *vis-a-vis* public, power play over the control of government, and the very meaning of the budgetary numbers and of the economic role of government. Is it meaningful to query whether there is anything but ideology to inform us as to how large or small the budget should be and/or of what it should consist? We economists like to talk of "rational" budgets and budgetary procedures and so on, but we are no more coherent or consistent than anyone else as to what rational means: whether we are referring to decisional structure, decisional process, or decisional results; or how to identify unequivocally a "rational" budget. Rational is like responsibility: a code word for whatever normative substance may be imputed to it. The reality is that there are different kinds of rationality and, especially, that government budgets are, unfortunately or not, a result of composite choice, including bargaining and similar processes, in which consistency itself is ambiguous or equivocal. It is a process in which ideologies of spending and taxation combat with each other. Our professional danger is that of over-intellectualizing a power process – one which has intellectual elements within it but which is not solely an intellectual process – and thereby of losing sight of what the process is all about while remaining a part of it. Of course, not all investigators are quite so uniformed. I guess the point is that budget making is inherently a normative process and *all* uses of "responsible" and "rational" are normative. The mantle of science cannot change this.

7. THE PROSPECT FOR LIBERAL DEMOCRACY

William A. Niskanen

> " . . . the government created by this compact
> was not made the exclusive or final judge of the extent of
> the powers delegated to itself, since that would have
> made its discretion, and not the constitution, the measure
> of its powers."[1]
>
> Thomas Jefferson 1798

7.1. Introduction

Is a liberal society compatible with democratic government? Can democratic states survive in a world of hostile governments? What individual and collective actions would improve the prospects for liberal democracy?

For the first 150 years of the United States, few Americans would have asked these questions, and the answer would have been self-evident. In the 1830s, a skeptical de Tocqueville asked whether democracy was safe for the world and received the characteristically pragmatic American reply, "It works!". Fifty years later, James Bryce reported that "'What do you think of our institutions?' is the question addressed to the European traveler in the United States by every chance acquaintance."[2] A flood of immigration testified to a world-wide perception that America was the land of the future. The American experience, for better or worse, has a way of transforming German socialists into midwestern Republicans.

American self-confidence probably peaked when the United States entered World War I to "save the world for democracy." Since that time, the prospect for liberal democracy has been progressively eroded by both external and internal conditions – the most important of which include the success of Communist armies,

---

1. Thomas Jefferson, "The Kentucky Resolution," *The Annals of America*, Vol. 4, (Encyclopedia Brittanica, Inc., 1968), p. 62.
2. James Bryce, *The American Commonwealth*, Vol. 1, (London: Macmillan, 1888), p. 1.

the Great Depression, and the progressive increase in the relative role of government in the democratic states. Only a few of the many national states formed since World War II have maintained a constitutional democracy. Only 20 percent of the world's population now live in the two dozen or so constitutional democracies. On the 200th Anniversary of both the political and economic blueprint for a free society, more Americans are questioning the viability of our institutions than at any previous time.

Analysis must precede prescription. But the perception of a problem must precede analysis. American political analysis atrophied as a consequence of the unrivaled success of the American experiment. As problems accumulate, however, pragmatism is not enough. As a political community, we are at sea without a rudder; we do not share a theory that explains both our success and the reasons for our developing problems.

The primary conclusion of this essay is that there is a fundamental flaw in the Constitution of the United States and of other constitutional democracies. If this flaw is not recognized and repaired, the processes of democratic government will probably destroy the basis for both a liberal society and democracy. And, finally, the "constitutional revolution" that is necessary to preserve liberal democracy must transfer the distribution issue from the political agenda to the constitutional agenda.

Some definitions are in order at this stage. A society is defined as a group of people subject to a common set of rules or laws. A liberal society is characterized by a set of rules that minimize the sum of the costs of coercive actions by individuals, by the agent enforcing the rules, and by individuals and agents "outside the rules," subject to the equal application of the rules among individuals in the society. The primary role of government in a liberal society, in the words of the U. S. Constitution, is to " . . . secure the Blessings of Liberty to ourselves and our Posterity . . . ". A democracy is defined as a society in which the population has the fundamental authority to select the rules and the enforcing agent. A liberal democracy, thus, is a society in which liberal rules are selected by democratic processes. A liberal society requires some government but does not imply a specific form of government. A democratic government does not assure the selection of liberal rules. As it turns out, a liberal society is compatible with democratic government only under a very special set of conditions, and the prospect for liberal democracy is dependent on a recognition and re-enforcement of these conditions.

7.2. The Democratic Leviathan

What are the consequences of unconstrained democratic politics? Are these consequences even consistent with preserving the basic democratic processes? Alexander Fraser Tytler, an 18th century Scot historian, anticipated our contemporary concerns with gloomy prescience:

> A democracy cannot exist as a permanent form of government. It can only exist until the majority of voters discover that they can vote themselves largesse out of the public treasury. From that moment on, the majority always votes for the candidate who promises them the most benefits from the public treasury, with the result that democracy always collapses over a loose fiscal policy, always to be followed by a dictatorship and then a monarchy.[3]

It is interesting to reflect that Tytler's conclusion was based on his analysis of the democratic experiments in classical Greece, prior to any history of modern democracies.

The primary internal threat to liberal democracy is a totalitarian democracy. For our purpose, a totalitarian democracy is defined as a government in which a majority of the voters (or their representatives) may change any provision of the effective constitution other than the franchise and the election rules. In earlier articles, I have made the case that the primary political event of the last decade or so was the dramatic change in the effective constitution.[4] The democratic character of our institutions has proved to be remarkably invulnerable to oligarchic threats. The limits on the functions and powers of government that are a requisite for a liberal society, however, have been rather rapidly eroded by democratic processes.

It is useful to estimate the consequences of a totalitarian democracy for several reasons — to provide a base case against

3. Quoted in Sir John Glubb, *Soldiers of Fortune*, 1973, pp. 229–230.
4. W. A. Niskanen, "The Pathology of Politics," Richard Selden (Editor), *Capitalism and Freedom: Problems and Prospects*, (Charlottesville: University of Virginia Press, 1975), pp. 20–35.
W. A. Niskanen, "Public Policy and the Political Process," Graduate School of Public Policy Working Paper No. 29, June 1975, Berkeley, California.

which to judge the present conditions, and to identify those processes that limit the democratic leviathan. The major unique process that limits the potential of a democratic government to exploit the minority is voting. The other major types of individual behavior that limit the exploitive potential of any form of government are the reduction of taxable income and exit. These processes are explored below in this order.

A. Voting

Voting provides substantial protection for any group included in the franchise, if their interests are effectively represented. First, consider the redistributional consequences of the following conditions:[5]

- All heads of households are included in the franchise and are equally represented in government decisions.
- All voters vote their own economic interests; i.e., they have no marginal benevolence (or malevolence) to others. (The assumption that there is no malevolence is important: Lebanon, Cyprus, and Northern Ireland are examples of the consequences of democracy with malice.)
- All government decisions are made by majority rule.
- The effective constitution allows collective transfers, subject to the constraints that transfers to lower-income families can be no lower than to higher-income families and the marginal tax rate on lower-income families can be no higher than on higher-income families.

And, in the first case to be considered,

- The elasticity of supply of taxable income is zero.

Table 1 presents the consequences of democratic redistribution under these conditions, given a pre-tax distribution of income that is roughly representative of the United States.

---

5. These are essentially the same conditions explored by James Buchanan, "The Political Economy of Franchise," Richard Selden (Editor), *Capitalism and Freedom: Problems and Prospects*, pp. 52–77.

Table 1. Democratic Redistribution Given Pre-Tax Income

Coalition	Percent of Money Income by Quintile					Transfer Budget
	1	2	3	4	5	
(0,0,0)	41.0%	24.0%	17.5%	12.0%	5.5%	0.0%
(3,4,5)	23.4%	23.4%	23.4%	18.0%	11.7%	19.0%
(1,2,5)	34.5%	24.0%	17.5%	12.0%	12.0%	6.5%
(1,3,4)	39.8%	23.7%	18.0%	12.5%	6.0%	1.5%

The first row presents the distribution of income in the absence of any taxes or transfers.[6] The second row presents the post-tax and transfer distribution of income resulting from a coalition of the lower three income groups. This coalition generates a transfer budget of 19 percent of total income and marginal tax rates of 100 percent in the top two income groups. The relative size of the transfer budget would increase as a function of the inequality of the pre-tax income distribution.

For these conditions, however, transfers are a zero-sum game, and there is no dominant coalition if all groups are equally represented. The two higher income groups can break the (3,4,5) coalition by offering to increase the transfers to the lowest income families. This reduces the transfer budget to 6.5 percent of total income and reduces the marginal tax rate of the highest-income group to 38.2 percent. The lower-middle-income groups, in turn, can break the (1,2,5) coalition by a further reduction in the transfer budget and the marginal tax rate. And the (1,3,4) coalition can be broken by the original (3,4,5) coalition. Any majority coalition favors some redistribution of income, but no majority coalition dominates all other majority coalitions. The potential circularity of majority voting, of course, is neither a surprise nor a general problem, because the consequences of different coalitions are usually similar. In this case, however, the consequences of the several potential coalitions are very different, so one should expect continuous political controversy on transfer issues.

This example may raise more questions than it answers about observed government transfers. Total government social welfare

---

6. The numbers presented are the estimated percentage of pre-tax, post (money) transfer income of families in the United States in 1973. For this anlaysis, the pre-tax, pre-transfer income distribution would have been desirable but is not available. U. S. Bureau of the Census, "Money Income in 1973 of Families and Persons in the United States," *Current Population Reports*, Series P-60, No. 97 (1975), Table 22.

expenditures in the United States are now about 20 percent of national income, but marginal tax rates are not 100 percent; this suggests that many social welfare programs should not be regarded as transfers among income groups but as tax-financed services to people in the same income group. We do observe that redistribution is a periodic (and often poisonous) political issue, but we do not observe enormous instability in the level of the transfer budget. Why have the higher income groups not been able to form a (1,2,5) coalition that would both reduce the transfer budget and increase the transfers to the lowest-income families? This is the potential coalition for a negative income tax, but there seem to be no early prospects for a break of the currently effective coalition. One possible explanation is ideological resistance on the part of both the rich and the poor to form a coalition on this issue. Another explanation is that both the rich and the poor are effectively disenfranchised by the geographic basis for representation, since the variance of the median incomes among Congressional districts is much smaller than among the population. This explanation suggests that proportional representation would increase the potential for a (1,2,5) coalition on distribution issues only at the cost of reducing the stability of any coalition. The primary lesson of this example is that voting protects the interests of the rich only when they are able to form an effective coalition with the poor. Any effective coalition that excludes the rich should be expected to extract from them the maximum potential tax revenue. The primary revolutionary threat to an unconstrained democracy is likely to be a "rightist" coalition of the rich and the poor.

B. The Supply of Taxable Income

The supply of income subject to taxation by a specific government, of course, is not invariant to the marginal tax rate. The generation of income is the result of individual actions and a social process, and tax rates influence income generation in several ways. An increase in the marginal tax rate should be expected to reduce hours worked, the formation and maintenance of human and physical capital, the relative employment in more onerous occupations and regions, the relative employment and investment in activities subject to low-cost monitoring by the tax authorities, and the relative employment and investment in the taxing jurisdiction. Any one of these effects may be small, but the combined effects are likely to be substantial. Moreover, the aggregate elasticity of supply of taxable income is likely to increase over time. The potential reduction of taxable income is the primary limit on the exploitive potential of any form of government.

For any individual, the tax rate that maximizes (gross) tax revenues is equal to $1/(1 + E)$, where E is the elasticity of supply of taxable income by that individual; (the tax rate that maximizes revenue net of collection costs is slightly lower.) If the elasticity of supply of taxable income by some individual is 1, for example, a marginal tax rate of 50 percent maximizes the gross revenues the government can collect from that person. A government is unlikely to set a higher rate except by mistake or malevolence.

In addition, we are protected by the differences in the elasticity of supply of taxable income among individuals. All of us who enjoy our work earn more than our reservation wage because others have a higher reservation wage. A government cannot know the elasticity of supply of taxable income of individuals; at most, a government can set rates based on an estimate of E by income groups and sources of income. As a consequence, most individuals in a tax rate group will be subject to a tax rate less than the revenue maximizing rate, because others have a higher elasticity of supply of taxable income. In a state with an exploitive government, the enjoyment of the finer (non-taxable) things in life is a public good. The rhetoric of all totalitarian governments is filled with exhortations against the "shirkers" and the "malingerers." Our liberty, however, is a function of our differences; both the puritans and the flower children should recognize how much they need each other.

Table 2 presents the consequences of democratic redistribution in a state where the supply of taxable income is a function of the tax rate. The conditions that generate these consequences are the same as those described above, except that the revenue-maximizing marginal tax rate is assumed to be 50 percent.

Table 2. Democratic Redistribution Given Maximum Tax Rates

Coalition	Percent of Money Income by Quintile					Transfer Budget
	1	2	3	4	5	
(0,0,0)	41.0%	24.0%	17.5%	12.0%	5.5%	0.0%
(3,4,5)	29.9%	21.4%	21.4%	16.5%	10.7%	17.4%
(1,2,5)	36.7%	22.8%	17.5%	12.0%	11.0%	5.5%
(1,3,4)	39.8%	23.7%	18.0%	12.5%	6.0%	1.5%

The first row again presents the assumed pre-tax and transfer distribution of income. A (3,4,5) coalition, in this case generates a maximum transfer budget of 17.4 percent of total income; the effect of a limit on the marginal tax rate on the high income group is to reduce the post-tax and transfer income of each other group. Although the maximum tax rate is limited by the elasticity of supply of taxable income, the rich still have an incentive to vote if they can form a coalition with the poor. These other coalitions reduce the total transfer budget but, again, there is no dominant coalition on transfer issues.

The potential for democratic redistribution is further limited by the demand for government services. If transfers absorb the total revenues generated by the maximum marginal tax rate, for example, any expenditures for defense and other services must be financed by either reducing transfers and/or increasing the middle-income tax rate. A demand for both transfers and services, of course, will generate lower levels of both transfers and services than if one or the other demand was not effective.

Table 3 presents the consequences on the distribution of money income and the level of the government budget in the United States for several combinations of transfers and services, given a maximum marginal tax rate of 50 percent. The first two rows are identical with those in Table 2. A (3,4,5) coalition is assumed to be effective on each issue. Both the level of services and the middle-income tax rate will be determined by the demand for services by the middle-income group.

Table 3. Democratic Financing of Transfers and Services

| | Percent of Money Income by Quintile | | | | | Budget | |
	1	2	3	4	5	Transfers	Services
Pre-Tax	41.0%	24.0%	17.5%	12.0%	5.5%	0.0%	0.0%
Transfers Only	29.9%	21.4%	21.4%	16.5%	10.7%	17.4%	
Services Only	29.3%	20.8%	17.5%	12.0%	5.5%		15.0%
Transfers & Services	27.8%	19.3%	19.3%	14.2%	8.3%	9.8%	11.3%

For this case, the demand for services by the middle-income group is assumed to be

$$Q_3^D = 15 (1 - C'S_3), \text{ where}$$

C' $\equiv$ marginal cost of services, assumed $= 1$

S_3 $\equiv$ marginal tax share of middle income group

For the assumed pre-tax distribution of income, a marginal tax rate of 50 percent on the two high income groups would generate tax revenues of 15 percent of income. If the *total* government budget is less than 15 percent of income, thus, the tax share of the middle income group is zero. For any budget larger than 15 percent, however, the marginal tax share of the middle-income group is 25 percent. For the assumed demand function for government services, thus, the budget for government services would be 15 percent of total income in the absence of any transfers and 11.25 percent of total income if tax revenues must cover both transfers and services. Similarly, the transfer budget would be 17.4 percent of total income in the absence of any services and 9.8 percent of total income if the government provides both transfers and services. A tradeoff between transfers and services is forced by the fact that any government budget above 15 percent must be financed by increases in the tax rates on incomes up to the level of the middle-income group.

This example has been designed to illustrate recent and present conditions in the United States. Twenty years ago, the federal budget was less than 20 percent of national income, most of the budget was spent for defense and other services, and the federal tax rates on lower-income groups were minimal. Since that time, the "transfer revolution" has increased the federal budget share of national income by about 40 percent, reduced the share for government services, and increased the tax rates on the lower-income groups. The increase in transfers has been financed primarily by reducing the relative expenditures for defense and reducing the relative income of those middle and low-income families not eligible for transfers.

This example, and my reading of present conditions, leads me to believe that the federal budget is about in equilibrium. A further increase in the relative transfer budget appears unlikely unless the demand for government services is reduced (or the revenue maximizing marginal tax rate is increased, possibly by a deterioration of conditions in other nations). Any increase in government services would probably be financed by a reduction of transfers and an increase in the middle-income tax rate. The "transfer revolution," I believe, has about run its course. The major present concern is whether democratic politics will generate a sufficient level of defense spending which, given the present transfer budget, must be financed by increases in the middle-income tax rate.

One interesting option suggested by this analysis involves breaking the (3,4,5) coalition on transfer issues. A (1,2,5) coalition would make possible an increase in the defense budget, a reduction in the middle-income tax rate, and an increase in the transfers to the lowest-income group. My guess is that this will be the platform of the next major political entrepreneur. This change necessarily involves a reduction in the transfers to middle-income families, but this may be the cost of maintaining an adequate defense in a hostile world. A democratic government can probably not finance both an adequate defense and a broad-based welfare system. There appears to be no fundamental incompatibility, however, between democratic politics, an adequate defense, and even more generous care of the poor.

C. Exit

The ultimate individual defense against a totalitarian government is exit. The opportunity to emigrate limits the power of a government to exploit any individual, even if he has no vote and he has a high preference for income subject to tax. The following relations hold for any individual:[7]

$$G_A + P_A + M_{AB} \geqslant G_B + P_B$$

$$G_A \geqslant G_B + P_B - P_A - M_{AB}, \text{ where}$$

$$G_A \equiv \text{value of government services in state A}$$

$$P_A \equiv \text{value of private services in state A}$$

7. This is a slight modification of the analytic framework in James Buchanan and Charles Goetz, "Efficiency Limits of Fiscal Mobility: An Assessment of the Tiebout Model," *Journal of Public Economics*, 1972, Vol. 1, pp. 25–43.

$M_{AB} \equiv$ costs of moving from state A to state B

$G_B \equiv$ value of government services in state B

$P_A \equiv$ value of private services in state B

All variables are in present value terms. An individual will remain in a state as long as the sum of the value of government and private services plus the costs of moving are greater than the sum of the value of government and private services in the most attractive alternative state. For some people, the opportunity to emigrate is not very valuable; the second relation suggests that an individual may remain in a state even if the value of government services is zero or negative.

Some further elaboration on several of the above variables is valuable. An individual's valuation of private services in state $A(P_A)$ is a function of the after-tax real income in state A, relations with family and friends, and attributes of the social and physical environment. And, similarly for P_B. The costs of moving from state A to state B (M_{AB}) will be a function of the physical distance and transportation costs, the quantity of unmovable physical capital and selling costs, the absolute difference between the language and culture of the two states, any exit controls in state A, and any entry controls in state B.

Table 4 summarizes the directional effect of these conditions on the value of government services to each individual.

Table 4. Conditions Affecting the Value of Government Services

Direction of Effect on G_A	
Favorable	*Unfavorable*
Government services in B	
Income in B	Income in A
Tax rates in A	Tax rates in B
Attachment to B	Attachment to A
	Distance from A to B
	Transportation costs
	Difference in language and culture
	Ownership of physical capital
	Selling costs of capital
	Exit controls in A
	Entry controls in B

The opportunity to emigrate, of course, provides the most discipline on the performance of a local government or state within a federal union in which there is a common language and culture and there are no controls on the movement of population and capital.

The opportunity to emigrate provides the least discipline on the government of a large rich nation in which family relations and private ownership of capital are important such as, for example, the United States. Most economic and social phenomena, however, appear to be changing in a direction that would make emigration a more attractive option and a more effective discipline on the U. S. government – the increasing relative income in other countries, the spread of an international English-speaking culture, the erosion of family ties, the reduction in transportation costs, and the increasing efficiency of the capital market. Governmental actions offset some of these effects: a reduction in the performance of government in other nations and the spread of movement controls reduces the discipline of the emigration option. Controls on immigration and capital exports, unfortunately, are very attractive to democratic governments, and such actions reduce the performance of all governments. Liberal government is a public good among nations, and some form of international constitution on population and capital movements could improve the performance of all governments.

7.3. The Constitutional Challenge

How did the problems of our constitutional democracy develop? Where do we go from here?

The primary contemporary problems of constitutional democracy, I contend, are the result of an extra-constitutional process of constitutional change. The national governments of the democracies now define their own powers, in response to the political processes affecting the decisions of these governments. The potential problems of a democratic government that defines its own constitution have long been recognized. Seth Low, writing to James Bryce, observed:

When . . . all men . . . are politically equal, and all men equally enjoy the right to take part in the government of a country, the experience of the United States would indicate that an omnipotent parliament would then be full of peril. The United States have enjoyed the measure of prosperity which they have had by trusting completely the whole of society. But written constitutions, in the nation and in each of the States, protect at once the individual, the State, and the nation, from hasty and ill-considered actions on the part of the majorities as to matters fundamental. Laws may be passed by majorities and may be removed by majorities, but majorities cannot change, in a moment, the fundamental relation of government to the people . . . To the American mind, it seems as though England's omnipotent parliament, which has been to her so valuable during this period of change from the feudal to the democratic ideal, may before long become an instrument full of danger to the state, unless, in some way, checks producing the same effect as those which have been found necessary in the United States are placed upon the exercise of its omnipotence.[8]

In the late 19th century, neither Low nor Bryce could conceive of the same problems developing in the United States, because of the American commitment to a formal constitutional process of constitutional change.

A century later, however, without any change in the enumerated federal spending powers, the powers of the U.S. federal government are almost unlimited. Congress has proliferated transfer, grant, and regulatory programs that have no formal constitutional basis. The flood of domestic legislation since 1965 has not even been rationalized in terms of the enumerated powers. The 10th Amendment, alas, appears to be only a "parchment barrier" to the extension of federal powers. All of Low's concerns about an "omnipotent parliament" have been realized in the birthplace of constitutional democracy.

For most of American history, liberal constitutional theory has held that the exercise of undelegated powers by any government is null and void. Several quotations illustrate this tradition:

. . . whensoever the general government assumes undelegated powers, its acts are unauthoritative, void, and of no force.[9]

Thomas Jefferson 1798

8. James Bryce, *The American Commonwealth*, Vol. 1, (London: Macmillan, 1888), pp. 567–568.
9. Thomas Jefferson, "The Kentucky Resolution," *The Annals of America*, Vol. 4, (Encyclopedia Brittanica, Inc., 1968), p. 62.

... the powers of the federal government as resulting from the compact to which the states are parties, as limited by the plain sense and intention of the instrument constituting that compact, as no further valid then they are authorized by the grants enumerated in that compact.[10]

James Madison 1798

... the government it created was formed to execute, according to the provisions of the instrument, the powers therein granted ... ; that its acts, transcending these powers, are simply and of themselves null and void.[11]

John Calhoun 1832

... if the subordinate body attempts to transcend the powers committed to it, and makes rules for other purposes or under other conditions than those specified by the superior authority, these rules are not law, but are null and void ... They ought not to be obeyed or in any way regarded by the citizens because they are not law.[12]

James Bryce 1888

The spirit of this tradition is that the language of the Constitution is clear and that every citizen has the right to interpret "the plain sense and intention of the instrument." The essence of a constitutional democracy is that the whole of the people is the superior authority and that the government is subordinate to the fundamental law defining the relation between the people and the government.

Against the background of this tradition, how have the several institutions created by the Constitution (Congress, the Presidency, and the federal courts) been jointly able to assume almost unlimited power to change the effective constitution? The powers of any one of these institutions have been quite successfully limited by the "checks and balances" of the other federal institutions, but there appears to be no effective limit on the combined powers of these institutions. My own reading of American political history leads me to conclude that this problem reflects a fundamental flaw in the Constitution, a flaw that has led to periodic problems that were resolved in the past in an *ad hoc* manner that deferred a more general recognition and correction of this flaw.

10. James Madison, "The Virginia Resolution," *The Annals of America*, Vol. 4, (Encyclopedia Brittanica, Inc., 1968), p. 66.
11. John Calhoun, "Address to the People of the United States," *The Annals of America*, Vol. 5, (Encyclopedia Brittanica, Inc., 1968), p. 577.
12. James Bryce, *The American Commonwelath*, Vol. 1, (London: Macmillan, 1888), p. 326.

The Constitution, in brief, does not establish an adequate procedure for forcing a constitutional test of the assumption of undelegated powers by the federal government. The Constitution (Article V) provides an adequate procedure for testing the consensus on any formal amendment proposed by Congress or a convention. Reflecting Madison's vision of a "compound republic," the Constitution also grants powers to the federal government (Article IV, Section 4, and the 14th Amendment) to guarantee a republican form of government and the civil rights of individuals in each state. The only procedure by which an individual or state can test the constitutionality of a federal action, however, is in a case brought before the federal courts. No procedure is established for forcing a constitutional test on issues for which the Supreme Court is unwilling or unable to enjoin the actions of Congress or the Presidency or of a decision by the Court itself. The Constitution establishes the Court as the only arbiter of constitutional issues, short of the formal process of constitutional amendment. The Constitution of our "compound republic" is asymmetric: A vote of the legislatures in one-fourth plus one of the states can block a formal amendment. There is no corresponding procedure for the same number of states to force a formal constitutional test by enjoining a change in the effective constitution.

The procedural solution to this asymmetry is as old as the Magna Carta and has been circulating in the backwater of American political theory since the beginning of our republic: some proportion of the parties to the constitutional contract must be able to enjoin the actions of the government established by the contract in order to force a formal constitutional test of the actions. Clause 61 of the Magna Carta established a group of 25 "guardians of the charter," any 4 of which could notify the king of violations of the charter and, if not resolved within 40 days, bring the matter to the other guardians.[13] This famous clause, probably the contribution of Stephen Langton, was subject to continuous attack by defenders of the royal prerogatives, and was omitted from later versions of the charter when the king gained power.

The Kentucky and Virginia resolutions, written respectively by Jefferson and Madison, tried to establish a similar procedure in 1798. These resolutions articulated the concept that the exercise of

13. *Encyclopedia Brittanica* (1972 Edition), Vol. 16, p. 579.

undelegated power had no force of law, but proposed nothing more than a common appeal by the states to Congress to repeal the Alien and Sedition laws. The election of Jefferson and a Republican Congress in 1800 led to early repeal of these laws but deferred consideraton of the basic constitutional issue. The South Carolina Ordinance of Nullification, written by John Calhoun, raised the issue again in 1832. This ordinance, declaring that the selective tariff on manufactures was unconstitutional and would not be enforced in the state, was designed to force a constitutional test on this law. This issue was resolved by Congress in the compromise tariff legislation of 1833. Although Calhoun recognized that some form of sanction was necessary to force a constitutional test, his argument, unfortunately, misdirected the earlier concept. Jefferson and Madison resisted the action by any one state to nullify a federal law; Calhoun declared the right of every state to nullify a law which it regarded as unconstitutional. Madison regarded the United States as a "compound republic" in which the states and the national government have a mutual responsibility to enforce the constitution of the other government; Calhoun declared the states to be "free, independent, and sovereign communities." Calhoun, unfortunately, confused the case for a collective responsibility of the states to enforce the federal Constitution with an unviable concept of "states' rights." The State of Wisconsin next raised this issue in 1859 to force a constitutional test on the Fugitive Slave Law, which required the return of slaves that had escaped. The Wisconsin confrontation with the Supreme Court was resolved only when a newspaper editor who had been arrested was pardoned a few days before the start of the Civil War.

The doctrines of "nullification" and "interposition" have been criticized or dismissed by later political theorists, primarily because they were later used to defend the institution of slavery and the continued denial of civil rights to negroes. Americans have an unfortunate habit, however, of evaluating a legal concept by the motivations of its advocates. Most contemporary Americans probably regard the Alien and Sedition laws, the protective tariff, and slavery as repugnant. The doctrine of nullification, however, should not be evaluated by the fact that it was first developed to attack bad law and later used to defend other bad law, but rather whether it would, in general, have promoted law that reflects the broad consensus of the population. The Civil War was the first

major tragic result of the failure to correct the constitutional flaw
to which this doctrine was addressed. The "constitutional anarchy"
of our time, I suggest, is the result of the same problem.

The prospect for liberal democracy, I contend, will be dependent
on some constitutional reform that would enforce a constitutional
process of constitutional change. This reform should build on
Madison's concept of a "compound republic." The federal government is now an effective guardian of the constitutions of the states.
The state governments, correspondingly, should constitute the
"guardians of the charter" of the federal government. Andrew
Jackson's response to Calhoun was correct in stating that the
federal union could not survive if each state could nullify federal
law. It is also important to recognize that a constitutional
democracy cannot survive the subjugation of any substantial
minority. The general nature of the constitutional reform that
derives from this analysis would be to authorize a group of states to
enjoin any federal law, executive action, or court ruling within
some specified period. A specific amendment to the Constitution,
consistent with these principles, would provide for the nullification
of any federal action by the vote of more than, say, one-third of the
state legislatures within one year after the date of the last vote. Such
an amendment would be designed to force a constitutional test on
any action, and would be nearly symmetric with the present
provision for approving constitutional amendments. Such an
amendment would provide a considerable period for both reasoned
evaluation of the federal action and continued federal abuse of its
constitutional powers, but it should protect the nation against both
an ephemeral whim and an indefinite extension of federal power.
The primary expected effect of such an amendment would be to
force a compromise that would avoid exercise of the nullification
authority on most issues.

A broad coalition, of course, is required to approve any
constitutional amendment. The federal government has abused its
powers, however, because the actions serve the interests of a
substantial part of the population. The central problem for the
advocates of constitutional reform to restrict the powers of the
federal government is to gain the approval of those who now
benefit from the abuse of these powers. Whether or not the federal
actions that created these benefits are regarded as constitutional,
the beneficiaries of these actions must also be included in any new

constitutional consensus. The redistributive genie is out of the bottle, and no amount of wishful thinking will convince people to relinquish the transfer dividends from their voting rights, without compensation. A constitutional consensus must be based on the status quo, not some status quo ante. For this reason, any constitutional reform to restrict the powers of the federal government, I believe, must be paired with a constitutional agreement on transfers and taxes. The amount and character of the redistribution that is, in some sense, "right" from a moral or efficiency perspective is irrelevant in this case. The necessary distribution is that which will achieve a constitutional consensus on both constitutional process and redistributive issues. The prospect for liberal democracy is dependent on moving both the process of constitutional change and redistributive issues from the political agenda to the constitutional agenda. Neither the tory skeptics nor the romantic democrats are right; democracy is not doomed to either failure or success. Our collective future as a political community will be of our own making.

COMMENTS

Martin Bronfenbrenner

Speaking as an economist, an undergraduate political science major, and an ex-law student, I congratulate Bill Niskanen on yet another extraordinarily ingenious contribution to the interdisciplinary development of these three disciplines. And while I think some of our disagreements are substantial, they may be no more than discussant's quibbles.

To begin with, I agree with Bill's underlying pessimism about the probable future of liberal democracy of the American constitutional type. My reasons for pessimism parallel those of Heilbroner's *Human Prospect* rather more than those of this paper, but there is no real conflict. As the Japanese say, "Many paths lead to the summit of Mt. Fuji."

The paper is too short to explain as fully as Bill may have wanted, why our republic did not collapse so rapidly as, say, John Adams and Lord Macaulay thought it would, once the suffrage had been extended to the proletariat. I myself see little of the explanation in the mechanical paradoxes of voting among income quintiles, as compared with five vaguer sociological considerations:

- The high U. S. living standard, compared with the pervasive Communist and Fascist down-grading of consumer interests.
- The high U. S. social mobility, real or imagined, which seems to induce people to vote their anticipations or their "deserts" rather than their present conditions.
- The fractionation of the U. S. proletariat along racial, linguistic, and religious lines.
- The appeal of freedom as such, emphasized by the media, the educational establishment, and other U. S. agencies of propaganda and public enlightenment.
- The high prospect of getting what one wants economically by inflationary bargaining about wages, prices, and profit margins.

Bill and I both believe that "a democratic government cannot finance both an adequate defense and a broad-based welfare system" in today's military technology and today's "rising entitlements." He is more confident than I about there being "no fundamental incompatibility between democratic politics, an adequate defense, and . . . generous care of the poor." For these reasons, particularly the last, he sees the strongest threat to liberalism in a "Tory-democracy" or "quasi-Fascist" demagogic alliance between the richest and the poorest (his quintiles 1,2, and 5). Possibly influenced by Cold War politics, "Director's Law," and books like Djilas' *New Class*, I envision at least equal danger from a Communist-Socialist-meritocratic alliance of Niskanen's income classes (2,3,5), or (2,4,5) against the very rich and some elements of the labor aristocracy. (Incidentally, I wish the parade of coalitions on Bill's Tables 1–2 had included these alternatives – and also, perhaps the entire group of seven combinations ($_5C_3$ - 3) which he decided to omit.

In the manner of a drowning man grasping at straws, Bill proposes to take America half-way back to John C. Calhoun – concurrent majorities and nullification – and likewise to Jefferson and Madison of the Virginia and Kentucky Resolutions. He wants it made possible for 13 State legislatures to enjoin for a year any Federal legislation, executive order, or lower court decision, pending a definitive declaratory judgment by the Supreme Court as to its constitutionality. To me, this savors of "gimmickry" for several reasons:

— It would require a constitutional amendment in view of the post-Calhoun history, and such an amendment seems extraordinarily unlikely of passage.
— It would involve the constitutional testing by the present Supreme Court and not John Marshall's. This implies to me that many Federal activities which Marshall and Niskanen considered and consider unconstitutional would pass muster under contemporary interpretations of the "commerce" and "general welfare" clauses of the Constitution.
— A good many State legislatures tend toward both venality and dilatory tactics. Some do not even have regular annual sessions. It seems relatively easy to hold off nullificatory action for a year or two in such States.
— A related possibility is log-rolling of the following sort. In State A, rapacious trade unions (teamsters, building trades) are strong, but agriculture is weak. In State B, rapacious farm organizations (dairymen, tobacco growers) are strong but labor is weakly organized. It should be little more difficult for the farm and labor leaders to cooperate across state lines to block the Niskanen scheme than it has been at the Federal level.
— Not only average incomes but income distributions are becoming more similar as between States. If an anti-liberal coalition of the Niskanen type operates nationally, may it not also do so within each individual State?
— The Niskanen proposal seems to me to increase rather than reduce uncertainty for business, agricultural, labor, and other economic interests. A greater volume of potential legislative and judicial sand is introduced into the economic gears and wheels. I wonder whether Bill has taken account of the economic consequences of this aspect of his proposal, or whether he disagrees with my conclusion about uncertainty?

I should not expect the Niskanen proposal to operate retroactively to re-test, for example, any aspects of the Roosevelt New Deal which I think we both regret. The proposal could also be used, rather, to block *repeal* of much special-interest legislation we would both like to see repealed. So I shall end this comment by venturing into counter-factual history to consider a few pieces of recent legislation and guess how his proposal might have affected them "long, long ago, long ago."

It would have blocked much New Deal farm and labor legislation, unless the farm and labor lobbies could already have cooperated across state lines. It might have permitted the "tax colony" and "old folks' home" States to block increases in Federal income and estate taxes, and retain a few more loopholes. I don't see how it would have blocked inflation by either fiscal or monetary routes; State legislatures, too, are averse to voting for taxes or opposing appropriations – and oppose high nominal interest rates on principle. The Niskanen proposal would not, I am sure, have prevented the Korean or the Vietnamese wars, the Cold War and the subsequent detente, or the several tergiversations of what are politely called our Soviet and China policies. What it might well have blocked is foreign aid, freer trade, poverty, and civil rights legislation. While no partisan of foreign aid in particular, I am not convinced that this package of blocks and delays would have helped liberal democracy on balance. It might instead have accelerated the migration of the poor to the Northern cities, exacerbated urban problems, and permitted the race riots and disturbances of the 1960s to blossom into the "black revolts" and "black revolutions" the radicals were calling them at the time. I may be an "F-" student of conjectural history, but these are among the points which worry me with the Niskanen proposal.

Robert D. Tollison

When I first read Niskanen's paper, I was very enthusiastic about his proposal to return the power of constitutional sanction to state governments. My original inclination was to devote my comments to extending his discussion of the principle of nullification. For example, to make the nullification power of states in his proposal fully effective, one would have to improve the technology of voting in state legislatures so as to insure a response to federal action within his one year time constraint. Or, I would question his criticism of Calhoun for getting the principle of nullification off the track by stressing the veto power of one state, i.e., states' rights. After all, this is only a suggestion of a unanimity rule where one state can nullify a federal act, and in the context of Calhoun's original discussion of nullifying a tariff, such a system might work very well. It would at least give consumer states the chance to buy goods at least cost wherever possible, and if one state had veto power over a tariff, then this might well be a powerful device to promote competition and free trade.

But the more I thought about it, the more I decided to take an alternative tack in commenting on Niskanen's paper. I will thus concentrate my remarks on exactly how Niskanen's proposal fits into the theory of constitutional choice, especially emphasizing the distributional implication of starting the process of constitutional change from the point of where our constitutional system presently resides. I should also note that although I will not review Niskanen's political arithmetic, his paper stresses that some groups of people transfer income to other groups in exchange for political alliance, and as a result of the income transfer, the coalition is able to gain political power.

I am left uneasy by Niskanen's proposed solution because he recognizes the weakness of the system of checks and balances. As long as constitutional provisions for checks and balances are effective, there will be offsetting tendencies within the federal government. But the government *as a whole* tends to gain in power over the individual (Niskanen, p. 170, last paragraph). If this is the case, then why would providing an additional check through state approval of federal actions lessen the total power of government to encroach upon individual liberties? I would think that from his own argument Niskanen might conclude that such a proposal would merely be a method of making state governments more powerful along with the increases in power of the federal government.

I am more inclined to search for an answer along the lines suggested in Buchanan's *The Limits of Liberty*.[1] At the level of constitutional decision making, no group knows who will assume political power, and all groups may favor a liberal constitution. When particular political groups are then awarded the post-constitutional government via election, they will have incentives to usurp as much power from the people as possible. That is, the group in power would always extract the total "gains from political organization" at the post-constitutional level. The only way that society could return to liberal organization is through the writing of

1. J. M. Buchanan, *The Limits of Liberty* (Chicago: University of Chicago Press, 1975).

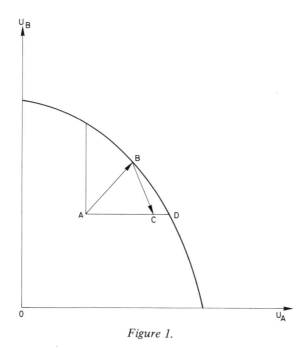

Figure 1.

a new constitution, and the trick is to devise a liberal constitution from which deviations are strongly sanctioned.

Let us examine the problem in very simple and suggestive terms. Figure 1 depicts the ordinal utility levels of two individuals along each axis. Point A represents an original anarchistic equilibrium, and movement to point B depicts one of the possible bargaining vectors along which these two parties could proceed to internalize the gains from a constitutional agreement. Suppose that, now, in the post-constitutional setting, the U_A's assume political power and begin to exploit this power to capture gains through existing political organizations. Movement from B in this case might proceed along a path such as BC. This path lies inside the $U_B U_A$ locus in the sense that original constitutional principles have been violated and checks and balances have not come into play to limit the exploitative activities of the U_A's. In this case the U_B's may tolerate constitutional erosion up to some point along AD, but at that time they would be better off in anarchistic equilibrium than by allowing further exploitation by the U_A's.

But what now? The basic choice seems to me to be that between starting at C and considering changes (such as that proposed by

Niskanen) in the existing constitutional system, which has degenerated along path BC, and returning to the anarchistic equilibrium at A and reconsidering movements to the constitutional locus. Movements from C could, of course, return the system to the constitutional locus, but given that the U_A's are rational maximizers, it would be an agreement with a distributional bias weighted toward those who originally exploited the constitutional principles agreed upon at B. On the other hand we have no guarantees that movements from C will be toward the $U_B U_A$ locus. An advantage in returning to the anarchistic equilibrium at A is to stress the need for consideration of returning to the constitutional locus and staying there.

There is, of course, no definitive answer to whether constitutional revision should start at a point such as C or A. C is not an unbiased point because of previous exploitation of constitutional principles by the U_A's, but it is the point where the system presently rests, and constitutional change must start from somewhere. It is my judgment, however, that by going back to A, which might be characterized as abandoning the present constitution entirely, we have the best chance not only of reaching agreement on liberal constitutional principles, but also upon mechanisms to insure the survival of such principles.